Refuge in the Storm

Personal Stories of God's Faithfulness

Compiled and Published by
Dick and Elizabeth Peterson
Mark and Cindy Woodard

ISBN: 1539834867
ISBN-13: 978-1539834861

ACKNOWLEDGMENTS

To our friend, Ed "Doc" West, whose painting, "Refuge in the Storm," is on the cover. To Crossroads Community Church Pastor Peppy DuTart whose challenge to multiply talents birthed this book. And to the contributors, whose walk by faith and not by sight revives hope in us all.

CONTENTS

INTRODUCTION

"Let the redeemed of the LORD tell their story—those he redeemed from the hand of the foe" (Psalm 107:2 NIV).

We all have stories. Those of us who are redeemed have stories of our Redeemer, how he bought us out of slavery, and how he pursues us when we slouch with dull memories of the old life toward the shiny trinkets of the marketplace. He holds us in his arms when we or those we love catch the scent of death, and he leads us home when we breathe deep.

Life in our Redeemer's care holds promise of beauty for ashes, joy for mourning, and praise to envelop the spirit of heaviness. The pages of this book tell about beauty, joy, and praise in the personal stories of people who know their Redeemer lives, because they encounter him—some of them daily. His faithfulness confirms his presence, and his power stays the hand of the foe.

A Sunday in August the lesson was the parable of the talents. Our pastor's illustration was a $10 bill for each adult, $5 for each youth and $1 to each child. "Go and multiply your talents," he told us. Elizabeth Peterson with Mark and Cindy Woodard discussed the idea to pool our talents to publish a book. The idea developed as a way to multiply our respective $10 talents and to multiply our God-given gifts and skills to give the redeemed a way to tell their story. I went along—a good idea, after all.

Mark and Cindy are pros at self-publishing. Elizabeth, the grammarian, is a great motivator to get people to write their stories and send them to me, the editor. Staring into a computer screen is my safe haven, and my spirit soared with the stories I read, transcribed, edited and wrote—stories that bear witness to God's faithfulness.

There's revelation in writing your story and release in telling it. Write it down and discover what's there. Enjoy the freedom of sharing your discoveries, and feel the warmth or your Master's approval as he says, "Well done."

Richard E. Peterson
Crossroads Community Church
Summerville, South Carolina

I AM GOD'S TREASURE

When I was a little girl, I was fascinated with the rainbow in the sky after a cleansing rain. After all, someone told me that if you just found the end of that rainbow, there would be treasure to be had—a pot of gold.

I grew up in a rural area of Chester, South Carolina. My grandfather, Pap, had a 1950 Chevy pickup truck. We had good times flying down the old country roads with me looking for a rainbow and him singing his favorite songs like "My Darlin' Clementine," and "I'm Looking Over a Four-Leaf Clover." I adored my Pap. He convinced me that one day we would find the end of that rainbow, and we would be rich from the treasure we found.

Those days did not last forever like I wanted them to. The rainbow treasure faded from my childhood dreams at the age of 12. My mother died of cancer, and I had to grow up fast. My three younger brothers needed a mother, and I thought I could wear those shoes because I was tough. My daddy seemed to be so distant and he missed my mama so much. She was Daddy's most beautiful rose. I know that because on the day she died, Daddy sat me down and told me that God had walked in his big garden that day and decided to pick his prettiest rose and take it home with him—my mama.

Daddy was never the same after that, and instead of turning to God, he turned to the bottle—alcohol bottle. Yes, my life changed, but not for the better—that I could see.

The way I looked at life and the world was different for me. My lenses were clouded with loneliness and never thinking I was loved—truly loved and special to anyone. I was always on the outside looking in.

We moved from my happy place on the big clay hill in Chester, where I

9

loved to see the rainbow and eat the big juicy red tomatoes grown in that red clay. We moved to be raised by my daddy's mother in North Charleston.

My grandmother was a no-nonsense, church-going, choir-singing, go-to-church-every-time-the-doors-open, godly woman. She made sure my brothers and I were in church. Girls' Auxiliary, Royal Ambassadors, sword drill, Ridgecrest, Training Union—all things Baptist was my life after that.

You would think that as many times I heard that God loved me, it would get rooted in my heart, and I would believe it. But I didn't. The years went by and I had two beautiful children and two broken marriages. I met both husbands in church, but I made wrong choices.

In my early 40s, I became a student of the Word and a woman of prayer. The Lord became my "safe place" and "my refuge." While studying Scripture one day, I came across Matthew 6:21: "For where your treasure is, there your heart will be also."

My mind went back to being a little girl chasing the end of the rainbow, looking for that treasure. I could see the pattern of my life until that day always looking for something precious, but never being able to find it.

"What am I missing, Lord"

"Where is your treasure, Ann?"

What? Is the Lord asking me where my treasure is? As I began to meditate on that Scripture, I decided to deflect that question to the one who created all things big and small. "Where is your treasure, Lord? Surely it is Jesus."

In the total silence, and in awe of my God, I heard these words as clear as the tinkling of a bell: "You are my treasure."

My heart was broken and opened that day, and my life forever changed. I finally believed—my heavenly Father loves me just the way I am with all my hurts and warts and bumps in the road. No more searching for the end of the rainbow. I found my treasure in Jesus' love for me. His love for me is real and more precious than any pot of gold or anything this world has to offer.

Ann Almers

'For where your treasure is,

there your heart

will be also."

Matthew 6:21

OUR WORST DAY, OUR HAPPIEST DAY

Isaiah 55:8 *"For My thoughts are not your thoughts, nor are your ways, My ways,"* says the Lord.

We received the call in December of 2009 telling us Jim had colorectal cancer. The next few days were a whirlwind as we had to meet with an oncologist, radiologist, and surgeon. At the time, all three doctors told us the same thing, "hopefully this is just a small tumor and surgery will take care of it."

At the same time, our first grandchild, a boy to be named Davis, was a couple days late in making his earthly arrival. Both of my brothers and my sister and all of their families were here from out of state to visit for Christmas and hopefully would be here to welcome the first great nephew into this world. God's provision and protection came that day in giving me the courage I needed to tell our children their dad had cancer. I was especially concerned of how our oldest, full-term pregnant daughter, would take the news. It was absolutely amazing to have my siblings here to help comfort our children, while Jim and I were busy going from one doctor to another and trying to process all of the information we were given.

By January 2, 2010, baby Davis was taking his time and had still not arrived. All my siblings headed home. Jim's parents were here and going to stay for a while. Our daughter was told her labor was going to be induced on January 5 if the baby did not arrive before then. I was still very optimistic and kept telling everyone, myself included, that I believed Jim's cancer was going to be an easy fix. After all, three doctors told us this was a curable cancer. Jim was scheduled to have an internal ultrasound at 8 a.m. January 6. This scan would tell us exactly how big

13

the tumor was and what stage the cancer was in.

Our daughter's labor was induced as planned. I stayed with her all day at the hospital waiting. Nothing happened, so by 8 p.m., the doctors decided to let Jess have some food and a good rest, then try again the next day.

My head began to scream, "Wait! Jim's scan is the next morning, at a different hospital, 45 minutes away!" At this point, I was talking to God nonstop, only it wasn't what I would call prayer. It was more like a question session for me, "Okay God, what exactly am I supposed to get here? Are you really going to let me miss the birth of my first grandchild? Jess needs me, but so does Jim. How can I do this?" My mind was so busy working, I didn't take the time to stop and listen to God, something I had done poorly for the past year.

Jim's procedure went as planned and the doctor, who was a straight to the point kind of man, walked in the room and his exact words to Jim were, "I hate to tell ya, but you're gonna have to be bagged (his term for a colostomy), the cancer is stage three, touching the lymph nodes, but we won't know if it's in them until after you have surgery. You're going to go through hell on earth to beat this, but it is a beatable cancer as long as it isn't in the lymph nodes."

Jim was only 47 years old, we had just had our 24-years wedding anniversary a week prior. It seemed as though my world fell apart, but I couldn't let Jim see it. I became a queen at the put-on-a-happy-face game even though I felt like this was the worst day of my life.

Eight hours later, I was reminded, his ways are not our ways, as I watched our first grandchild take his first breath. God knew what he was doing when He turned the worst day of our lives into one of the happiest days of our lives.

Jim did go through 10 months of pure torture after that to beat the cancer that had invaded his body. Having little Davis in our home every day, gave Jim the joy he needed on those tough days, to push on. Davis was our sunshine on many cloudy days and we continue to thank God for giving him to us.

Almost seven years later update: We are celebrating 31 years of marriage, we now have a 5-year-old granddaughter too, and praise God, Jim remains cancer free.

Margo Black

"For my thoughts are not your thoughts, nor are your ways, my ways," says the Lord.

Isaiah 55:8

HE GIVES, TAKES AWAY, BLESSES ABUNDANTLY

We thoroughly enjoyed the 33 weeks God allowed us to carry our son, Robert David Branton Jr., and we treasure the opportunity God graciously allowed to hold him in our arms. During those weeks, as God was forming his little body, we grew to love our son more, and we have no doubt that he sensed our love as we sensed his.

What a masterpiece of God's handiwork! Our imaginations were satisfied as we touched and admired him. He was definitely a "Jr."; he looked just like David—round face, double chin, big nose and all.

Excellent medical care and a perfect, by-the-book pregnancy into the middle of the eighth month could not prevent the umbilical cord from narrowing where it entered his body. It is at this weak point that the cord twisted and crimped. Only Christ, who formed him in secret, could know and control this.

We don't pretend to understand or have all the answers, but our faith is in Jesus Christ, and we trust him. Still, we have to ask, Why?

Jean Branton

Our arms are empty, and the loneliness does not go away. Emptiness visited again when we miscarried Robert David, and still again when our twin sons, Stephen and Scott, remained with us for only a few hours.

Why? is always tough. It's not to question God's authority, his ability, his wisdom, or his right to claim his magnificent creation, but to question: What can I learn about God from this?

I believe God asks us, "Do you love me?" He asked us when our first son died, when we miscarried, and when our twins raced ahead of us to be with our heavenly Father. "Then, prove it." We proved it to ourselves and to God with each passing. Our answer: "Yes, Lord, I love you. You know that."

His challenge: "Then, prove it to the world." When we ask him why, that's his answer, and whatever that means, we will prove it to the world one day, one minute, one second at a time.

We're not powerful, but we serve a supernatural God, and he covers us. He covered before and he will cover us again. Our God is too wise to be mistaken, too good to be unkind. When I can't see his plan or trace his hand, I can only trust his heart to know that he has a plan and he is working it out.

Even if this experience of having children is all God ever allows us, we consider ourselves fortunate. We are proud parents with many happy memories (and a scrapbook too!).

David Branton

"For I know the plans I have for you, declares the Lord,

plans for welfare and not for evil, to give you a future and a hope. Then you will call upon me and come and pray to me, and I will hear you.

You will seek me and find me, when you seek me with all your heart."

Jeremiah 29:11-13

MY TRUST IS IN THE LORD

I had a nightmare that I was running from the police, but when I thought about it, what was I really running from?

In the nightmare, I came to a park that had a well in the middle of it. I started to climb down into the well, but when I was near the bottom, I couldn't see anything. It was pitch black. It was deep and coming from the bottom were roaring noises that scared me so much I climbed back up. When I got out of the well, a crowd of people with the police had arrived, and in front were my mom and dad. I called, "Daddy." He backed away. "Mommy?" She backed away too.

The police told me to get out of the well because it was too dangerous. I didn't know what to do, so I climbed halfway back down into the well. I was scared, and asked, "Why, God?" When I looked down into the pit, heard another roar, and then woke up.

When my mom and dad came to me, I told them about my nightmare. Dad said it would never happen again, but if it did, he would help me. Mom told me that I should read a chapter in the book of Daniel, but she said I didn't have to if I didn't want to.

Later that day, I grabbed my mom's Bible wanting to read the chapter in Daniel, but before I found it, I remembered the day before my mom had bought a Christian movie from Redbox named "Miracles from Heaven." The movie is about a girl who had something wrong with her stomach. She had to go through so much pain that it made me cry. Halfway through the movie I stopped it and decided to find the chapter in Daniel.

When I found the chapter, there was an index card with a verse on it from Philippians 1:6. It said "for I am confident of this very thing that he who began a good work in you will perfect unto the day of Christ Jesus." I flipped the index card over and saw the reference of another verse, John 15:11. I found it and it said, "I have told you this so that my joy may be in you and that your joy may be complete."

I felt like a couple of pieces of the puzzle had come into place. I decided to finish the movie. The little girl was healed because she trusted God. I went back to my mom's Bible and read the chapter in Daniel. I realize now that Daniel was alive because he trusted God.

That day I decided to put all my faith and trust in the Lord.

Ashley Britt

"And I am sure of this,
that he who began a good work in you
will bring it to completion
at the day of Jesus Christ."

Philippians 1:6

THROUGH IT ALL THE LORD IS WITH US

Two years after retirement as a police officer, Jim created a new career for himself as a fire investigator and was doing very well. We had life under control.

At that time Jim was dealing with this sinus issue that had been an annoyance for several months. He had been to the doctor and given a couple medications (which he doesn't like taking) which offered no results. One day he decided to stop at a "Doc-in-a-box" Urgent Care on his way to investigate a fire. When they called us with some test results, we were in a church meeting and missed the call. Since they were open late we decided to swing by and pick up what we thought would be a new prescription. We didn't get one, what we got was "Mr. Carl, you have stage four "CLL" Chronic Lymphocytic Leukemia." All we heard was: Leukemia!

Life just took a new turn.

As we drove out of the driveway in tears, I remember very strongly the Lord saying "It's going to be okay." *Okay? How can this be okay?* My mind started going through these mental negotiations with Him. *Wait a minute. My childhood life was a mess. I lost my mom when I was 17; lost my hero dad at 31; my brother was a mess and died a couple years later. My immediate family was gone. Haven't I done my time? Really. Leukemia?*

Working as an administrator at our church, my friend and Pastor Barry Arnold was a source of reason. I couldn't even bring myself to discuss this with our twin daughters. How do we tell them? We've worked all their lives to protect them from the ugliness of this world and this just doesn't fall into our plan. Our plan? Who do we think we are? Our plan, not God's plan? Barry said, "You have to tell them." In a way, I felt we had neglected them for so long by protecting them from the real world.

We did some research, and decided that we would do whatever we could do to fight this disease. We pulled out the big guns and contacted a friend of ours, a professor of medicine at the Oregon Health and Science University. If we were going to go down this road, we were going to drive a Mercedes.

Jim started chemotherapy and handled it pretty well. He was still able to continue his new-found profession and we had hope.

Success! After the five months of chemo Jim was cancer free. Yeah, that wasn't fun and I'm glad it's over.

After a little over a year, I noticed Jim's neck getting bigger again (glands). Our biggest fear came to play—its back. This is a cancer, that they told us is slow growing, and it's back. People who get this are usually older and don't even need treatment. Then there's always that exception to the rule.

They're doing great strides with bone marrow transplants and Jim's a candidate. They sent us information about the process and, in a very nice colorful brochure, it mentioned some of the side effects to the procedure called GVHD, graft versus host disease. It's a condition where the incoming cells beat up the diseased cells causing issues with the organs. They offered suggestions to help cope with these problems. I studied them very carefully and bought everything I could in preparation.

December 23, 2010, we received news that there was a donor and Jim received his bone marrow transplant. At 2 a.m. the IV was placed and after 15 minutes, Jim did just fine and the doctor left. This was easy! Everything went well and as planned. We slept through the rest of the night and were home to celebrate Christmas as a family.

One month later, Jim had extreme skin pain. If I touched him, he would be in incredible anguish. That was it; I had to take him to the hospital. Thankfully, the Lord put our good friend Tony at our door step when I was trying to load Jim into the car. We got him to the hospital and within three days, Jim had lost all the skin off his back and his thighs. They weren't sure whether to keep him there or send him to a burn unit.

Sparing the day-to-day details during this time, during one of the doctor visits I met them in the hallway and asked, "What should we expect?" They told me he has a 20 percent chance of surviving. I think they were being kind. They didn't expect him to live.

Our Cornerstone Church family (Gresham, Oregon) was amazing! They broke into prayer. The kids sent enough handmade cards to fill his hospital room with color. The visitors were encouraging, and the amount of support was overwhelming. God's people were our strength and the post we leaned on. After 33 days, we went home.

Wish I could say this was the end of our saga. In mid-July, Jim woke up and said, "This is strange, I can't see out of my right eye." In layman's terms, he had a stroke behind his eye and had permanently lost vision in that eye. An old, very well respected eye doctor who had many interns following him like he was Paul McCartney, examined Jim. He, very gently, said, "Your eyesight is gone in this eye. But that's why the Lord gave us two eyes."

This isn't what we wanted to hear; we'll just have to work with it, it's not like we have a choice. Jim was still able to do his fire investigation work. In addition, there were some other GVHD issues to deal with.

Labor Day weekend Jim came in from outside. He sat on the bed and looked at the floor. "What's wrong?" in my heart of hearts I knew, and it didn't take long for him to confirm my fear. The other eye was going.

We could get him to the doctor as an emergency. That was it. He would be totally blind within two days. Barry and another elder rushed there to anoint Jim and pray with us and the girls. Life just took another turn. A big turn. You just can't prepare for this.

Living in a split-level house, our home, didn't work well for a blind man. After falling down the stairs we knew we had to move. The Lord, not only put the right property in our path, He put all the right people there too. We were able to build a one-level home with no stairs with an amazing group of people who packed us up, unpacked us and continue to watch over us. This will always be a tremendous testimony of God's universal family.

We want to be willing to accept the path the Lord has for us, but there are times when life's overwhelming experiences leave us numb. We know the Lord is with us. We've watched people who have been touched through this journey. We can see why He brought us through these trials. We've always prayed that the Lord would use us for his kingdom. We just forgot to give him our preference list: Maybe a missions' trip, feed the homeless, take care of the elderly—all wonderful deeds. Never, ever did we want to be the ones to be served. No! We want to serve others. Even at this ripe old age of 60, we continue to learn, His way is right.

Jim and Polly Carl

"Trust in the Lord with all your heart
and lean not on
your own understanding"

Proverbs 3:5

DELIVERED TO MINISTER

I knelt on the bedroom floor praying for deliverance. A full-length mirror in front of me reflected the sad woman I was. I crawled over to my purse, took out a makeup lipliner and began to write on the mirror. Sad. Hurt. Tired. Broken. Depressed. Forgotten. I backed away and begged the Lord to bring peace and healing: *Lord, take away the pain in my heart so I can be all you created me to be for your kingdom.*

As I continued to look into the mirror, Isaiah 58:8 came to mind—not the verse, the reference. I didn't know what the verse said, I only know the Lord gave it to me, so I ran to my Bible, opened it and read aloud. I sobbed so hard I could barely breathe. I knew at that moment the Holy Spirit was present; I felt the Lord's peace surrounding me.

Still on my knees, I crossed out and wrote beneath each word who I was in Christ. Joyful. Loved. Victorious. Healed. Worthy. I could feel the strength of the Lord rise up in me. As I wrote out the verse the Lord gave me, word by word I claimed the beginning of a new life: *"Then your light shall break forth like the morning, your healing shall spring forth speedily, and your righteousness shall go before you; the glory of the Lord shall be your rear guard"* (Isaiah 58:8).

I received Christ when I was 15. I know the Lord is with me, but the enemy knows it too and fights hard to bring chaos into the lives of those who belong to the Father. Choices, oh the many choices. I look for choices that would mold me into a woman of God. As a teenager, I was an unwed mother. I didn't know who my earthly father was, and I've suffered rape, divorce and illness.

But over the years the Lord has led me into ministering to women, and it was while I was preparing to speak at a women's conference that I had another encounter with the mirror.

"I really ought to clean it," I thought. Then came the still, small voice that said: *No, use it for the conference.* So, that's what I did. Overwhelmed at God's timing and the sweetness of that morning several months back, I hauled the mirror to the church, set it up on the stage and reenacted what the Lord did for me when I was in despair and crying for help. I shared how he delivered me from the pain, heartache, stress, and worry that had been making me physically ill.

My light broke forth that morning. My healing began and in time I was much better. My righteousness—which is the Lord—went before me and delivered me that morning, and the glory of the Lord has been my rear guard ever since!

Today I am happily married, and God in his grace has given me three children, a step-daughter, two sons-in-law, a daughter-in-law to be, four grandsons and granddaughter due to arrive in a few months. I share my story because the Lord has blessed me immensely and my life is beautiful. I am grateful and thankful for His grace and mercy.

Tabitha J. Crocker

It was on a summer day in June as I watched my hero, my confidant, my best friend—my mom—slowly take her last breath. Watching in shocking dismay, my heart filled with grief and anger. She was leaving me. Who would listen to me and not judge me? Who would give me godly advice? Who would I call on my way home from work?

As one great woman left my world, another great woman came into my world. A transfer of care was being passed through my mother's prayers. It was as if she was passing the baton to my new best friend, Tabitha.

God's timing always reveals that he has a purpose and plan for my life. Waiting on this revelation has not been easy for me. The day after my mom's funeral I was sleeping on her couch. It was as if I could hear her voice again saying, "Mike, you are going to be fine."

God always has a way of providing peace in the most difficult times. My wife, Tabitha is my mom's answered prayers. She is my best friend.

Michael E. Crocker

"Then your light shall break forth like the morning, your healing shall spring forth speedily, and your righteousness shall go before you; the glory of the Lord shall be your rear guard"
Isaiah 58:8

AN ANGEL TO GUARD ME

One day in 1999 I was not feeling well, and my husband John was getting ready to go to work at the sheriff's office. I told him I didn't feel well, and at that moment I collapsed. I quit breathing.

John called 911 and two first responders from the fire department arrived, applied the defibrillator, shocking me twice before I started breathing again on my own. They transported me to Summerville Medical Center Hospital, where they stabilized me and then told John they were going to transport me to Trident Hospital where they were better equipped to handle this type of heart attack. A nurse told John not to worry, and she was going to ride with me to make sure I would be okay.

I didn't know anything for two weeks. The doctors told me that I would not remember anything that happened and for me not to worry about that. When I could ask John what happened, he explained it to me. John said that Pastor Peppy had come, and everyone was praying for me. There were a lot of ladies from my Sunday school class, and they were praying for me also. John explained everything that happened from when the EMTs arrived at the house, and about the nurse who rode with me to Trident Hospital.

I told John I wanted to thank everyone and wanted to meet the firemen that saved my life and the nurse that rode with me to the hospital. I finally got to meet the two firemen. There was a dinner that was being held to honor some of the firemen and EMTs for their work for the past year, and we were invited to attend. John and I presented a plaque to them for saving my life.

John and I went to Summerville Medical Center Hospital and met with the supervisors who were working that night, and they told us there was no nurse who could have ridden with me. The only people who can ride are the patient and the EMT personnel.

I feel that God is still using me and that he still has my guardian angel by my side. All the prayers put out in my name have helped me make it thus far.

Peggy Decker

"For he will command his angels concerning you to guard you in all your ways"

Psalm 91:11

SEEING CLEARLY NOW

I grew up in the church and was saved at a young age, but I didn't have any understanding of what a relationship with God meant. My parents didn't have much time for me, because they were spending most of their time either fighting with each other, or lecturing my older sister, so I quickly learned to deal with things on my own. I believed that I only needed my parents to clothe me, feed me, and put a roof over my head. I dealt with my school work and any internal problems on my own. I was taught, through my parents abandoning me, to either lock all my emotions inside, or completely ignore that the problems even existed.

Like most people, I compared my relationship with God as the same as my relationship with my parents. If I needed my parents for anything, they were there, but if I could do without them, I would. Sure, there were times I cried out to God, mostly in times of extreme pain or loneliness. But I tried to be in control of everything, and only cried out to God when I really needed something, which was not often.

I never realized that seclusion from my parents would result in fear of abandonment as an adult. That fear would lead me down a path of bitterness, resentment, and codependence. I became a drug addict, which only furthered my seclusion. It allowed me to ignore the pain I was feeling. Because I had an escape in drugs, I felt I was in complete control of any internal issues I was going through. I was going to school, making good grades, and I had a boyfriend who loved me, but I had a deep hole full of emotions that I was trying to fill with drugs. I believed it was working.

Due to over 12 years of drug addiction, I never grew up emotionally. I ignored the pains of my youth through the mask of fog I lived in. I was scared and felt completely alone in this pit I had made for myself, and for the first time in my life, I felt completely out of control and wanted someone to turn to for help. I had spent more than 30 years of my life doing things on my own, and I finally realized it wasn't working.

I turned my drug addiction over to God, and he graciously delivered me. He showed me that I needed him daily, and I needed to find a new way to live my life. Even though there were brief moments in my 12 years of addiction that I would wake up, I never tried to fill that void with something else. It always came back. It was exactly like the parable of the empty house.

After God delivered me, I started attending Celebrate Recovery. I discovered how emotionally stunted I was, and how much anger, bitterness, and resentment I still held in my heart from my parents. I learned through CR—and am still learning—how to let go of those hurts and grow up spiritually. It was a hard process, but I wasn't doing things alone anymore. I had God's help, and help from others with CR, along the way. This was something completely new for me, to actually let someone else help me.

I don't regret the decisions I made, because those decisions taught me valuable lessons. They taught me that I am not in control the way I always thought I was, and that I do not have the strength to do things on my own. God will give me more than I can handle so that I learn to rely on Him to get me through the storms. God gave me the tools to change the way I was living my life, so that I would fill my life with him instead of leaving room for the drugs to return. I need Christ in every part of my life, and He loves me more completely than I will truly ever understand.

Aleisha DeYoung

"No temptation has overtaken you that is not common to man. God is faithful, and he will not let you be tempted beyond your ability, but with the temptation he will also provide the way of escape, that you may be able to endure it."

I Corinthians 10:13

A NEW START ON A STRAIGHT PATH

When I was 8 years old, I prayed and asked Jesus Christ to be my Lord and Savior. At this age, I understood the message of salvation, but it wasn't until much later in life that I understood what this new life looked like and what it meant in terms of daily application.

My father accepted his first job as pastor when I was 12 years old. This started a season of intense pressure. This pressure came from the expectations to be a good preacher's kid at church and from stress at home. As the child of a preacher, I rarely had other adults to talk to about stress in my life and I quickly learned to keep everything inside.

This practice of keeping things to myself, made dealing with issues at home even more difficult. My mom was ill and stayed in the bed most of the time and my dad became emotionally detached. He often used her happiness to control me. My dad had high expectations for everything and I felt as though I could never achieve his standard of perfection. This led to a great deal of hidden resentment over the years.

The resentment I carried eventually started to be expressed through outbursts of anger and I spent my high school years grounded. Each time I was in trouble, I would apologize and seek their forgiveness. Over time, my parents started telling me that they didn't forgive me because I wasn't sincere and that they didn't trust me. At one point, my dad even told me, "parents equaled God."

I didn't understand at the time, but this statement was exactly how I viewed my relationship with God. I believed His approval of me was based on my behavior and if I messed up he would never forgive me. I basically believed that I had to be perfect for him to love me just like it seemed my parents expected the same. This subconscious view fueled my rebellion.

Over the next few years, I stopped going to church and started down a path of turning to all the things that I said I would never do. The most influential of these rebellions was the choice to use drugs to hide from life and responsibility. At first, I believed I could control it, but over time, I was using all day, every day. I spent nearly 12 years of my life using some form of drug. During this time, I held steady jobs and even got married, but drugs were nearly always there behind the scenes, taking over more and more parts of my life. There were periods of sobriety where I would attend church and wake up to some degree, but these periods were always done on my own power and I would eventually return to drugs to fill the void and hide the pain. God was using these times to teach me to see him differently and to realize that I couldn't do it on my own. After years of trying to be in control, I realized that I needed his help and I started praying earnestly for a change.

One day, after months of prayer, God in his mercy gave me another opportunity to turn from my drug use. I was determined not to waste this precious gift. I needed to learn to live in a new way. I reached out to my local church and I joined Celebrate Recovery. I have learned that God is willing to meet me where I am and that he loves me no matter what I have done or will do.

It took something like drug abuse to teach me to reach out to God and others for help and how to live my new life in Christ. It is more than just head knowledge; it is a relationship built for daily application. I need Christ in every part of my life and he loves me more completely than I will ever truly understand.

Jeremy DeYoung

"For by grace you have been saved through faith. And this is not your own doing; it is the gift of God, not a result of works, so that no one may boast. For we are his workmanship, created in Christ Jesus for good works, which God prepared beforehand, that we should walk in them."

Ephesians 2:8-10

FINDING WHAT'S MISSING

I was born in a suburb of New York City around World War II. My parents loved neither themselves nor me, which fed the resentment I built up against them and my brother, who they treated differently.

Several times in my life I felt so broken I thought I'd never be made whole.

My father, who was in the Air Force, wasn't a part of my life until I was about 12 or 13, and I felt the brunt of the discord between him and my mother. Never feeling loved took its toll on my life.

My mother kept me in church during the week and all day on Sunday, especially. She was a mean woman, always beating me with ironing cords. I had to wear sweaters and leggings to cover the welts on my arms and legs. I was abused by relatives and some of my mother's friends, and by the time was 17, I had enough. I certainly didn't want any more of the church with its hellfire and damnation.

Through the years of uncertainty, I married and had children, but there was something missing. I eventually lived with just my children. I finally decided to try church again, which led to my dedicating my life to Christ, sometimes falling and getting back up again.

I can't remember when it was I told the Lord, I want to trust you with my life, but I have not turned back since no matter what. I am so happy to be walking with the Lord today, and I would not exchange the life I live now for anything or anyone.

Mabel Diamond

*"…I know the plans I have for you,
…plans to prosper you and not to
harm you, plans to give you hope
and a future."*

Jeremiah 29:11

POWER TO FORGIVE

When my youngest, Ethan, was six months old, I was in a car accident, which broke my right wrist and elbow. With the broken arm I was not able to lift him or take care of him.

My mom moved in with us for two months to take care of Ethan and our other two kids while my husband Ted was at work. Ted took care of the kids in the evenings. I had to quit nursing Ethan and wasn't able to put him to bed. This was something that I had done with my other two for the first year of their lives.

I was angry that I was not able to do the same with Ethan, especially since he was our last baby. I was angry at the man who hit our car. I was angry that his careless moment could change our lives so much and not affect his life at all.

I couldn't vent my anger at the guy I thought deserved it, so anyone in my path caught it, mainly my husband and children. I was short tempered, impatient, I yelled at them, and was in a generally bad mood all the time.

Ted suggested to me numerous times that I should talk to a counselor, but I refused to go. After all, I deserved to be angry. About four months after the accident I did finally meet with a counselor. My bad mood and anger was not going away and family life was stressful.

The counselor summed my anger in one word: Unforgiveness. I was angry because I would not forgive the man who hit me and changed my life. I needed to forgive him. She said that every time I thought about the man, I should pray to forgive him. In the beginning, I may need to ask God a hundred times a day to help me forgive the man, but one day I would notice that I was asking less and less until I had truly and completely forgiven.

It took awhile. There were many days it felt like I was asking God to help me a hundred times, but I did come to forgive him. And while I was in the process of forgiving him I noticed my anger was fading away. I became happier and more joyful. I enjoyed my family again. I was patient with them again.

In hindsight I can see other blessings. Ted got to put Ethan to bed while he was still a baby, and was able to bond with him in a way he didn't with the other two. Ted and I have a closer relationship with my mom now that we would not have if she had not lived with us for a couple of months.

Being able to let go of my unforgiveness also allowed me to let go of my anger and restore my relationship with my husband and kids the way God intended.

In Matthew 18:21-22 Peter asks Jesus how many times he should forgive someone who sins against him and asks if it should be seven times. Jesus answers, "Not seven times, but seventy-seven times." I've always looked at that verse as saying we should forgive someone many times even if they continue to do the same thing over and over.

Now I think in that verse, God also means it may take seventy-seven, maybe more, prayers for help to forgive before we truly have forgiven them.

Karen Gillgrist

"Then Peter came up and said to him, "Lord, how often will my brother sin against me, and I forgive him? As many as seven times?" Jesus said to him, "I do not say to you seven times, but seventy-seven times."

Matthew 18:21-22

WATCHING GOD AT WORK

It was like sitting in my grandfather's lap and hearing him whisper that it's going to be okay. "Everything will be fine. Just watch." It wasn't a voice, but I heard it. I understood it. I knew it was the Lord speaking to me.

My husband Dennis, and 9-year-old daughter Meghan were near death following a fiery auto wreck on March 7, 1999. Exiting our subdivision on a Sunday afternoon, their sedan was hit broadside by a pickup truck running a red light. The impact crushed Dennis' side of the car into Meghan's and propelled the car into oncoming traffic waiting at the stoplight.

When I arrived at the scene, I saw what looked like charred tinfoil in the road. When I saw the license plate, I thought I had lost my husband and my daughter. Meghan was transported to the Medical University of South Carolina Trauma Center by helicopter. Dennis was transported by ambulance.

As a friend drove me behind the ambulance, a thought surfaced: "If you trust me, it'll be okay." That nearly audible thought cradled me; it calmed my fears. It was as if I heard him ask if he was worthy of my trust. I could only answer, yes, and God, you are in control.

Later that afternoon and evening the word spread throughout our church's congregation: Pray for Dennis and Meghan. There's been a terrible wreck. Our church held me up with their prayer and descended upon us with such concern and care that the group grew to the size of a small congregation. They stayed late into the evening tracing progress reports and praying.

"If you abide in me, and my words abide in you, ask whatever you wish, and it shall be done for you" (John 15:8).

As the days passed Dennis continued to recover, and Meghan opened her eyes. She began to recognize her family. But the day I will never forget was the day one of Dennis' clients—Dave Davis, a pastor at Harbor Bible Church—read a funny children's story to Meghan. She smiled and giggled. It was so good to hear her laugh again.

And now, every day there's something new. I just get up in the morning and ask: What's new for me today, Lord? God is so good even when we don't have the faith to trust him. I remember praying for the Lord to increase my faith. My friend told me she heard me say, "My God is bigger than this. and if I trust him, everything will be okay." I'm sure he meant whatever the outcome.

I didn't know if they would recover, or if I would have to look to God to be my husband and a Father to my children, Chris and Melissa. I just knew God was in control and would take care of us all. I don't want people to say, "God took care of you, but my child died, or my husband is gone." I now know that he makes all things beautiful, and that he wanted me to trust him to do what's best in light of eternity.

I don't know what God has in mind when he allows things like this to happen, but I do know that the accident and the results of prayer let people see God at work.

Genie Gore

"If you abide in me, and my words abide in you, ask whatever you wish, and it shall be done for you"

John 15:8

THE LORD IS ENOUGH FOR ME

"The prayer of a righteous person has great power as it is working" (James 5:16b).

In 2005, during the aftermath of Hurricane Katrina, my friends, family and church were watching a storm ravage my life in Summerville, South Carolina. The last prayer I prayed was for the people of Louisiana, including my promise to God that no matter what happened in my life, I would trust him to provide all my needs. The next morning, I woke up with a high fever that resulted in a two-month intensive hospitalization. As the battle for my life began, my church family clung to the Lord like hanging onto a tree trunk while the wind blew us horizontally.

Hemophagocytosis was the eventual diagnosis reported to the CDC. The hematologist said the chance of it happening to me or to anyone is like lightning striking someone on a sunny day. It normally occurs in children under the age of 10. I was 46 years old. When the white blood cell count elevated, the white cells began "eating" red blood cells. The low red cell count caused four organs to fail. I was on life support, in a coma, and on a liver transplant list. Mine was one of four cases in the country at that time.

To complicate matters I had allergic reactions to the antibiotics. Friends told me I was unrecognizable. My body "blew up as big as the bed." I had a "red rash from head to toe and blisters that oozed." I was so swollen that my "eyes were like yellow slits" and I "looked like an alien." People were not convinced it was me in that hospital bed.

The church rallied and prayed for me. Their intercession broke through the ceiling of this world, entered the throne room of heaven, laying my sick bed at Jesus feet. My "numbers" began turning around and my organs began functioning again. Having almost died twice, I only remember hearing the sound of the most beautiful orchestral music.

When I was first coherent, the five specialists on my case came to my room on separate occasions. They stood in the exact same place and spoke the exact same words, "I did not think you were going to make it." My records are marked "spontaneous remission." The day my hematologist released me, he stood with three pages of blood work in his hands. Looking down at the pages, he said, "I'm 99.9 percent sure this thing is gone and I did not heal you." Six months later, the other three cases in the country were still in the hospital undergoing bone marrow transplants.

There are times in life that things are experienced for which only God can take credit. The Lord showed his power to many people when he miraculously healed me while I slept. Although recovery was painful and difficult, the purpose for what my body endured was for the benefit of others. It was not about me at all. And the people—they were blown away. If it became necessary, will he do that for me again? Whether or not he will, I know he can. And that's good enough for me.

Susan Greene

"You are the God who performs miracles; you display your power among the peoples."

Psalm 77:14

HE PREPARED A WAY BEFORE ME

I have been blessed to know Jesus all my life, being surrounded by a loving Christian family. Jesus became my personal Savior and Lord when I was very young. I knew he loved me and I never wanted to displease him (John 3:16).

There have been many trying times in my life, as with everyone, but one that tested me the most was losing my husband Jim. I went from caring for my parents to caring for Jim (Ephesians 5:25).

My story is about the way God orchestrated our lives. He prepared the way before we knew what the future would bring (Philippians 4:19).

God's path led us to South Carolina in 1983, leaving our oldest son, jobs, family, and friends in New York State. The move was especially difficult for our younger son who was starting high school (Psalm 4:8).

I enrolled in the College of Charleston to get my teaching certificate for South Carolina. This led to a job at Spann Elementary School. My income went for college tuition for our sons.

Jim's health began to deteriorate in February 1989. He was hospitalized for a week with blood clots. "Nothing is going to happen today, Lord, that you and I cannot handle." This was preparation for what was to come. (1 Peter 5:7).

Cancer was diagnosed in July. No hope. No treatment will help. He was given three to six months to live (Hebrews 4:16).

Jim had to quit work in August. Thank you, Lord. I have a job. We made Todd's last tuition payment in August. Praise the Lord (Isaiah 40:31).

My folks moved to South Carolina in April, 1989, and built a log home in Moncks Corner. They came to stay with Jim while I worked. I made provisions for a substitute teacher to meet my students so they would be taken care of when I needed to be out (Psalm 23).

By then Jim was bedridden. Hospice came to the house to help care for him and us. Dr. Hibner came to the house each week to see him. On one occasion, I remember both the doctor and his wife, who was also his nurse, gathering around his bedside to pray for him.

Our pastor also came to see him each day and had communion with him. During one of those visits he and Jim planned the funeral. Jim asked him to use John 3:16 for the message and to include the song "Amazing Grace."

There were times when Jim would become agitated and incoherent. During those times, I would begin to repeat Psalm 23 and he would join in with me.

Family from New York and our son from Columbia came to help, then Hurricane Hugo hit September 21. A tree smashed into our house taking out two of the bedrooms. Rain rushed in. Eight of us and two dogs rode out the storm huddled together until Hugo passed.

A friend provided a generator; electricity was restored. Insurance came through quickly and another friend had his company repair the roof.

Jim passed away on October 14. At 48 years, I was alone. Half of me was missing. My sons were out on their own. I lost my dog. I looked up to heaven and asked, "Now what, Lord?"

The Lord stepped in and I grew closer to him through my tears. The song, "Through it All," by Andrae Crouch, "I've Learned to Trust in Jesus, I've Learned to Trust in God," and the hymn, "Great is thy

Faithfulness," got me through many hard times.

Today I am humbled with what God has done and continues to do in my life (Ecclesiastes 3:1). Over the years, he has blessed me with grandchildren and great-grandchildren.

Skip Hanson

"For everything there is a season, and a time for every matter under heaven."

Ecclesiastes 3:1

WE LIVE BY FAITH

When I was 9 years old my parents, my brothers and sisters attended a little church in a little town in Ohio where I grew up. I sang in the children's choir, was in Sunday school, and in the youth group. The pastor gave an altar call one Sunday morning at the end of the sermon. I went to the altar that morning. However, my life took a turn down the wrong path after I graduated from high school.

My life was full of ups and downs. My choices of friends and my walk was not the best. I got married. My husband then and I had a beautiful little girl, Tina. We divorced after seven years of marriage. I came to a point in my life where I was miserable.

At the age of 25, I decided to join the military. I thought I needed a change in my life. I was searching for something but wasn't sure what that was. My four years in the Air Force was a great experience for me. I got to travel and see different places and I loved my job. I was stationed in New York where I was a Flight Scheduler at Wing Headquarters. I met my husband who was also stationed at the airbase. He was a tail gunner on B52 bombers. We dated for awhile then were married in New York.

Life was fun and full of adventure for my husband and me. We received our first set of orders for overseas to Osan, Korea. We were so excited to be able to travel together to another part of the world. Only a few months into our tour I became pregnant with our first child, a son.

At that time in Korea there was no base housing for families. the choice for families was to move off base or return to the United States. Moving off the base was not an option for us because it was not safe and you could not drink the water. The only option was to return to the United

States by myself and pregnant. My husband had to stay to finish his 12-month tour.

I received my orders to Utah, not where I wanted to go since I knew no one, and it was clear across the United States from my family. It was a long flight and I was traveling to a place I'd never been before and didn't know a soul. Once I reached my base I was given a sponsor to help show me around the base and community. I was fortunate to stay with my sponsor and their family who were so gracious to let me stay with them until I was able to find an apartment.

The first Sunday in Utah I decided to go to the chapel on the Airbase. It was Mother's Day and again I felt so lonely. I was in a place I knew hardly anything about and my husband was thousands of miles away. The days, weeks and months went by. In July, I gave birth to our son Keith. My husband missed the birth of our first son by a few hours due to trying to get a flight out from Korea. He was home for a few weeks then had to return to Korea for another three months before he would come home permanently. David and I had been apart for a total of seven months. Little did I know when he finally came home from Korea, our marriage would begin to slowly spiral downward.

After my husband had served his four years in the Air Force he decided to get out and get a job in a retail store as manager. I still had a year and a half left until I would retire from serving my four years. In that year and a half, I got pregnant with our second son David. My husband was a good father. He was always willing to help with the boys.

After my four years was up we decided to move to Florida where David's mom lived. We got a home and got settled. Our marriage continued to go downhill. We argued and couldn't get along. By the time the boys were 2 and 3 years old, I decided to separate from my husband and eventually we divorced. I felt sick, lonely and empty inside.

I began thinking about when I was 9 years old, the little church that I grew up in, the songs we sang in church, my Sunday school teachers and how I felt when I was in God's house. David began to pray for us.

I called him one day and asked him if we could go to church the next Sunday. He agreed. David gave me a Bible that had been his father's before his dad went to be with the Lord. I opened that Bible one day and it opened to Proverbs 31:10, "The Wife of Noble Character." As I began to read it, I started to weep. I felt something stirring in me I had never felt before. I prayed and asked the Lord to please restore my marriage, and promised that I would do anything he asked.

That Sunday I went to church with David and our sons. As the worship began with Amazing Grace, we stood and I looked at the cross hanging at the front of the church. I began to weep. The pastor gave an altar call. I couldn't get up the aisle fast enough. I realized I heard about God and always believed there was a God but never had a personal relationship with God. That's what was missing all this time. How can anyone have a relationship with someone, if you don't have a relationship with Jesus Christ first?

David asked me to marry him. I accepted. After David decided to reenlist in the Air Force, we had our third son Matthew. Today my husband is my best friend. After 37 years of marriage I can't imagine being with anyone else. To think we could have thrown a beautiful marriage away. God restored and healed our marriage.

Proverbs 24:3,4 says *"Through wisdom a house is built, and by understanding it is established; by knowledge the rooms are filled with all precious and pleasant riches."* How true this is!

In our home, there's a picture that hangs in our living room it says:

In this house, we give grace. We tell the truth. We make mistakes. We say I'm sorry. We have fun. We give hugs. We value family. We show love. We live by faith.

Marilyn Hunt

*"Through wisdom a house is built,
and by understanding it is established;
by knowledge the rooms are filled with
all precious and pleasant riches."*

Proverbs 24:3, 4

A REFUGE 2500 MILES FROM HOME

Proverbs 18:10 tells us, *"The name of the Lord is a strong tower; The righteous run to it and are safe."*

I have found this to be true so many times in my life, but one particular time in my life comes to mind right now.

When my three children were very small, my husband came home from work one day and announced that we were going to move from St. Louis to Seattle. After the initial shock, sadness began to set in. We were going to be leaving our church and our friends, and all of my very close-knit family. We would be 2,500 miles from my new home. I was a stay-at-home mom, and I was leaving all of my support group behind. We were moving somewhere that I'd never even visited, or even had a desire to visit for that matter.

There was so much to do, and since my husband, Jim, had to report to work, I was going to be doing most of it myself. I began sorting through the things we'd accumulated and packing up boxes of our belongings. We sold some of the things we no longer needed. I found renters for our house, and we rented a small house in Washington. Because they didn't allow pets, I had to find a new home for our cocker spaniel, Charlie. With each chore I completed, I became more and more aware that I was going to have to say goodbye and, honestly, I became angry as well as sad. My attitude was not good, to say the least! When moving day came that hot August morning, my parents helped me load up the truck and the children, and we reluctantly headed west.

I had left so much behind, but God was with me and I had plenty of time to talk to Him on the four and a half days it took to drive to Seattle. When we arrived at the little rental house, the neighbors on the cul-de-sac greeted us with warm smiles and Popsicles! They helped us unload the truck and then told us that their church was starting their VBS the next morning and our children would be welcomed to attend!

This was the beginning of a more than 25-year friendship. I found out later that our friends had been praying for Christian neighbors and were thrilled when we moved in. We were "adopted" by their extended family and spent almost every holiday with them. We had dinner together at least two or three nights a week. Even after we moved away, we have visited each other regularly and stayed in touch.

I'm so thankful for the friendship that God provided us. What a blessing they have been to us over the years! I learned this: when you're a Christian and you move, you never go alone.

Melonee Lechleiter

"The name of the Lord
is a strong tower;
The righteous run to it and are safe."

Proverbs 18:10

CASTING OUT FEAR

A few months after giving birth to my youngest daughter Myah in 2012, I started having severe panic attacks. I've always been a worry wart. I had been through some traumatizing experiences as a child and as a young adult, that most likely contributed to my anxiety issues.

I've always been afraid to go to the doctor because I'm convinced that the doctor will tell me I'm going to die soon. But this new anxiety and panic was completely different and life-changing for me. I physically felt like I was dying multiple times a day. I would get dizzy, off balanced, heart racing, disoriented, tunnel vision, feeling like I wasn't real or like I was in a dream. Depersonalization is what they call it, I guess. Never in my life had I felt so scared.

It started happening a few times a week to happening daily, to almost constant. I constantly had this feeling that I wanted to crawl out of my own skin. I had this severe uneasiness where I felt so uncomfortable I would just ask God that if it was my time to please just take me. I couldn't even sleep without waking up from having a panic attack. There was no escape.

I got to the point where I was too scared to go grocery shopping, too scared to drive for fear of passing out or losing control and causing an accident. It got to the point where I couldn't even take a walk down my driveway without feeling like the world was closing in on me. I was too scared to leave my house or even to get out of my own bed. I did, however, when I had too. I had three children to take care of, but the fear was overwhelming.

Agoraphobia is what it's called.

The worst part was my family could not understand. They couldn't understand why I couldn't just stop it. When I did finally go to the doctors, they found that my thyroid was not functioning at all. It was a relief to know that there was a reason I felt so bad and that it was treatable.

Postpartum thyroiditis was what I was finally diagnosed with. With some thyroid medication, I would be back to feeling like my old self, but that would not be the case and the easy fix I was praying for. It took four years of finding the right medication for me and even another diagnosis of Hashimoto's disease before I was physically feeling like myself again.

Through this journey of anxiety and panic attacks and the mental and medical causes for it, I feel closer to Jesus now than I ever have. I found amazing friends who understood and knew how to pray for me. There were some days I had to fully rely on God to carry me and get me through the day.

As a matter of fact, I had to listen to and sing the song "Carry Me" by Josh Wilson over and over again some days, just to get relief from the fear and pain I was feeling. I did learn that the song "Carry Me" was written because Josh Wilson also suffered from panic attacks.

Some Bible verses that helped me through this difficult time are: *"God did not give us a spirit that makes us afraid but a spirit of power and love and self-control"* (2 Timothy 1:7). *"We take captive every thought to make it obedient to Christ"* (2 Corinthians 10:5). *"I can do all things through Christ, because he gives me strength"* (Philippians 4:13).

It's been four years when this journey began. I went from being too scared to leave my house in Hallstead, Pennsylvania, to moving here in Summerville, South Carolina, 794 miles away from all my friends, family and church family. Even a year ago I could not have ever imagined packing up and moving so far away, but here I am.

I still have a hard time now and then. I'm still not feeling like the old me, but maybe that's a good thing. The old Stacy didn't pray as much and ask Jesus to carry her like the Stacy today does. God is good.......all the time. He has definitely carried me through the darkest days of my life.

Stacy Leeming

"We take captive every thought to make it obedient to Christ."

2 Corinthians 10:5

BEAUTY FROM ASHES

My life before Christ was a wreck.

I thought I was happy and for the most part, I believed I was. My sister and I were hurt emotionally and physically at a very young age through sexual molestation. Consequently, by the time I was 15, I thought I knew everything there was to know about being an adult. I left my mom's house and carried my past and my hurt, which had turned to anger, with me. For 18 years, I experimented with drugs, partied a lot, and started living my life as a lesbian, but questioned my sexuality. The first time I gave myself to a guy, I became pregnant with my daughter and gave birth to her when I was 17.

If you asked me then if I was happy, I would've said yes!

When my lesbian partner and I moved to South Carolina and I bought a house on a cul-de-sac, a friendly neighbor introduced herself and her family with a plate of cookies. We dog-sat for each other's dogs and made a pact that if either one of us needed anything day or night we would leave our porch light on.

I'd see her and her daughter on Sunday mornings leave in their car and return a couple hours later. It was their Sunday routine, and always with a book with frilly stuff around it in her arms. I had been warned that South Carolina was the Bible belt and I'd be judged, but when I got a job in a dental lab, I was open about being gay, and was accepted for my talent.

My neighbor, my job, no one judged me—not yet. I would have told you I was happy.

At work I noticed this guy who always had his pocket Bible and was talking about Jesus. I thought, this is the Bible belt guy my friends warned me about, and I decided to keep my distance. Whenever he came into my section of the lab, he'd say, "Hey Rosie, do you know Jesus loves you?" I'd say, uh…sure and walk away. He would remind me, "I'm praying for you." For five years we talked about work, family and other things, but he always referenced his pocket Bible.

I continued to watch my neighbor and her daughter on Sunday mornings. I'd go to the beach. That was my routine until the attacks of 9-11. My girlfriend had to return to New York to help her father and my daughter was off to college. Suddenly the most important people in my life were gone.

My neighbor's husband traveled a lot, and our pact to look out for each other included her promise to pray for me, and I knew she meant it. She started asking me to go to church with her and her daughter on Sundays. I'd say no thank you and go to the beach. *What's with these people, always talking about praying and going to church?* I was broken and every chance she had, she reached out to me. I was broken at work too, and along came pocket Bible guy asking if I was okay. *How could God love me and yet allow so much hurt in my life?* Once again I was angry.

The hurt and anger became so intense, one afternoon after work, I pulled my car into the garage, started it, said goodbye to my dogs, turned my porch light on and started walking through the kitchen toward the door to the garage when the doorbell rang. I tried to ignore it, but the dogs went berserk and the doorbell kept ringing. It was the guy with the pocket Bible.

Now I was really mad. "What are you doing here? How do you know where I live?"

"I don't know," he said. "I was driving home from work and God told me to find you. I was looking for your car. Where's your car, anyways?"

"It's in the garage. Why are you being so nosey? I'm busy." He told me he was afraid of dogs and asked if we could step outside on the porch. I spotted my neighbor go inside her house, later to find out she went inside and fell on her face in prayer for me.

There on the front porch, the rubber met the road. He told me how much Jesus loves me and wants me just as I was. I told him he didn't have a clue where I'd been and what I'd done. He said that God wanted me right there just as I was and loved me regardless.

We prayed together and I accepted Christ. God saw me as I was and loved me regardless. I rest in knowing *"There is therefore now no condemnation for those who are in Christ Jesus. For the law of the Spirit of life has set you free in Christ Jesus from the law of sin and death. For God, has done what the law, weakened by the flesh, could not do"* (Romans 8:1-3).

Seven years ago, God placed Allen, a wonderful, godly man in my life, who takes good care of me. I am a happily married woman, and yes, we go through trials together, but we know the hope we have in Jesus. For that I'm thankful. My life today is proof that *"...if anyone is in Christ, he is a new creation. The old has passed away; behold the new has come"* (2 Corinthians 5:17).

And the Lord laid out a new path for me that allows me to minister and share Christ with many who don't know him. I work as a deputy sheriff, the career I've always wanted. The Lord has made it clear to me *"And I am sure of this, that he who began a good work in [me] will bring it to completion at the day of Jesus Christ"* (Philippians 1:6).

Rosie Morris

"...if anyone is in Christ, he is a new creation. The old has passed away; behold the new has come"

2 Corinthians 5:17

HE HAS A PLAN FOR ME

On August 16, 2010, I walked out of the Good Neighbor Center homeless shelter for veterans and drove home with tears in my eyes. Why God? Why would you let my job come to an end? I loved my job as program director.

After losing my husband, the Good Neighbor Center was where my hope and happiness was restored. This was a ministry to provide hope to people in despair. I helped them find jobs and programs to overcome their drug and alcohol problems. I worked with churches that had Bible studies to encourage their spiritual growth. It was all so awesome. Suddenly I was in despair.

It was a new journey for me. I needed God's strength and comfort; what I had was anxiety over financial obligations and medical problems without insurance. The Ladies Sunday school class at Crossroads Community Church prayed for me daily. For the next four months, I applied for job after job, but depression set in and I began to lose hope. On sleepless nights, I'd repeat: *"To everything there is a season"* (Ecclesiastes 3:2).

On a Wednesday morning, a red bird (my little harbinger of hope, I now realize) appeared on my deck. *"Look at the birds of the air: they neither sow nor reap nor gather into barns, and yet your heavenly Father feeds them. Are you not of more value than they?"* (Matthew 6:26). And the MUSC Hospital director of Guest Services called to ask me to come in the next day to interview for a job. Later that week, I accepted the temporary job as a concierge in the Ashley River Towers working with families of patients with heart problems.

I still had no health insurance, but a medical doctor from Crossroads

Community Church offered to see me until I was able to obtain benefits. I worked two years until becoming a full-time employee with benefits. Later I transferred to the MUSC Trauma and Critical Care unit where I found my passion: helping families in crisis coping with loved ones in car accidents, suicides and gunshot wounds. Sometimes all I can do is just hold a parent's hand and hold the hope for their loved ones.

I look back on the journey and I'm reminded: *"For I know the plans I have for you, declares the Lord, plans for welfare and not for evil, to give you a future and a hope"* (Jeremiah 29:11). God has a plan that will lead to what is best for each and every one of his people. I may not always know or understand God's plan for me, but if I trust in him, he will lead me to hope. My heavenly Father performs miracles every day, and the beauty of the kingdom of heaven is more than I can fathom. One day it will be my home.

Faye Parker

'Look at the birds of the air: they neither sow nor reap nor gather into barns, and yet your heavenly Father feeds them. Are you not of more value than they?"

Matthew 6:26

A CALL TO REPENTANCE

I was not brought up in church. Somewhere along the line I did get acquainted with God and Jesus, though I didn't learn about them.

Coming from a dysfunctional family, my childhood and teenage years were as normal as can be, considering that due to mate-swapping, the three children in my family each had a different father. My first experience with sex was with a 26-year-old woman with three kids. My stepfather only asked if I had a good time. He wore a smile from ear to ear.

My military days were a different story. I learned to drink whiskey like a fish, and use women—married or prostitutes, it didn't matter—as disposable toys I found, had fun with and forgot. I thought this was normal. I was cynical toward people, disliked family holidays, and was a miserable person to be around.

Then I met a redhead who asked if I wanted to play pinball. I said something stupid, and nine months later she married me. For seven years, we tried to have a child. Finally, we gave up and decided to buy a new motorcycle. On our first trip to Kentucky, she became sick. When we got home, she found out she was pregnant, and she spent the following five months on bed rest. God gave us a little baby girl.

We had several conversations over a five-year period about going to church, but we thought we weren't ready to commit. A co-worker and Maurice, an older gentleman on a trike (a three-wheeled motorcycle), invited us to a biker Sunday. It was free, they provided lunch, and so I said, "Sure, I'll be there." My wife and I went and we decided to start going to church. We figured a good dose of morality would not hurt our daughter, and setting a good example, we showed up every Sunday.

On August 24, 2001, while on a charity ride for the Shriner's Burn Center in Cincinnati, Ohio, I saw several children with 80-to-90 percent of their bodies burned. A few had lost limbs. This should have made me sad, but that day I looked past all that and saw their spirit and how full of life they were. In fact, one little boy who lost both legs and one arm, tried to run me over with his wheelchair for his turn on a video game. I rode thinking and talking to God for the seven hours it took, stopping at the church. I went into the chapel and there I asked God to forgive me, and I asked him to be in my life.

Since that day, I've been baptized and have accepted Jesus as the Son of God who gave his life for our sins. I know this is just a starting point and that there are many challenges ahead, but with God working within, I'm never alone.

Bill Perryman

"For God so loved the world, that he gave his only Son, that whoever believes in him should not perish but have eternal life."

John 3:16

MY IDENTITY IS IN THE LORD

When the occasional weakness in my arms and leg and late-in-the-day foot drags happened more frequently, I asked for a referral to see a specialist.

At first glance, the neurologist didn't think my condition was serious and told me not to worry, but tests proved otherwise and a few days later, he called me to say the MRI showed lesions on my brain and spinal cord that indicated multiple sclerosis.

During the next visit my husband and I were told that there was no cure for MS, but statistics showed that only 20 percent of those diagnosed become wheelchair patients.

I was not one of the 80 percent who could keep my mobility and within the year, I needed a cane to walk down the hall at the school where I taught. Two years later, a four-wheeled walker, and then a power wheelchair replaced the walker. There was no doubt that I had progressive MS rather than relapsing remitting as the majority of patients have.

I grieved each loss and cried when I could no longer walk as I used to do so easily. I became both frustrated and angry when I could not open a jar or stand to reach an item from a shelf. Having to ask for help was and continues to be frustrating.

The biggest loss was leaving my job. It was one of the hardest things I've ever done. I'd wanted to be a teacher since I was a small child. When I was little, I lined my dolls and stuffed animals up in front of a chalk board and taught them the numbers and ABCs that my older sister had taught me.

I asked friends at church to pray for me to be able to teach in the classroom, telling them, "Teaching is my identity." They would nod and promise to pray. All the while, my heart was breaking and I was scared.

On one occasion, I asked a British missionary in our church to pray for me, and I shared with him how teaching was my whole identity. Instead of nodding in agreement, he began to shake his head saying, "No, you are wrong, Liz. Teaching is not your true identity. Your identity is with your heavenly Father."

That gentle correction helped me to admit both to him and to God that my sole identity was not in my job as a teacher, but rather in my heavenly Father.

We prayed together, I repented, and I renewed myself to being open to God's leading me, even if it meant leaving the job I loved.

That year I said goodbye to colleagues I had known for many years. I had peace that God was leading me to leave teaching in the classroom, and I prayed for him to show me what I could do while using a walker and wheelchair to get around.

I smile now as I remember those times of uncertainty and how God took care of filling my time just as he had filled me with peace about leaving my beloved career. First, I began praying each week in the prayer garden of our church with a friend who loves to pray. We prayed for others in the church, our families and for God to use me with my disabilities.

I saw a need for a support group in the Summerville area for people living with MS and I started a group in 2002 of fewer than 20 that has continued to grow to 35-plus attending monthly meetings. Several ladies from the church have come alongside me to help with the group and our prayers have brought many Christians to join the group.

When I had to give up driving completely, several homeschool parents asked me to teach Latin to their children in my own home. All the years in public school I had not been able to bring in scripture when I taught. I had wanted so badly to use the Latin Bible in my lessons but never could. Now, I had parents asking me to use Scripture.

One of my greatest joys was being asked to teach a Sunday morning Bible class of women. The promises of God took on new meaning. The new chapter I was stepping into would require believing that God could use me in my wheelchair with no ability to use my hand to write on the board or easily turn the pages of my Bible during the lesson. I am told that my disability encourages the ladies as they see God enabling me to teach from my wheelchair and depend totally on him for strength.

In the last year, I have added online teaching to my schedule. My husband helps me get ready for what we call "Prime Time" each evening and I help students with their homework or prepare them for a test.

MS changed me and the life I used to live. God had a plan for me that only he, as the master designer, could have conceived for me as I lost the use of my arms and legs to work as they had for so many years.

Each day I am reminded that my God is faithful and the words of Psalm 18:30 are a testimony to him. *"As for God, His way is perfect; The word of the Lord is proven; He is a shield to all who trust in him."*

Elizabeth Peterson

"As for God, His way is perfect; The word of the Lord is proven; He is a shield to all who trust in him."

Psalm 18:30

COUNT IT ALL JOY

My wife Elizabeth took the call. It was our daughter.

"Mom, we had an accident. Michael's pinned in the car."

I could tell from her expression; the call was serious. "They've had an accident on Butternut." Her terse statement was all I needed to go to them.

Butternut Road is the street our subdivision entrance spills into. I was there in minutes, praying audibly that God would bring glory to himself through this ordeal.

The call came late in the afternoon, January 15, 2011. My son-in-law Michael, daughter Kerry, and grandsons Michael IV, Andrew and Logan were returning from a local church-league basketball game. Grandson Michael's team won. The church gym was about five miles from home. They were almost to the entrance of our subdivision when an oncoming driver failed to negotiate a curve and plowed his Ford F-150 pickup head-on into their Chevy Suburban.

As Kerry tells it, she screamed, "He's going to hit us!" She says Michael veered to the right, but the pickup hit them on the left front, sending their Suburban into the trees.

Michael didn't remember any of it.

I had to park away from all the emergency vehicles and walk in, explaining to police and other first responders that was my family in there.

I spotted the children first. Logan, Andrew and Michael were sitting in a passerby's car waiting to be checked by EMS personnel and appeared to be scared, badly shaken, but not seriously injured. Kerry was on the roadside: "They're trying to get Michael out of the Suburban."

To avoid encountering the emergency crew working on the vehicle, I circled around from the woods-side of the crash site and saw them cutting away the door post and prying loose sections of the interior that had him pinned. He was unresponsive.

Michael was airlifted by helicopter to the Medical University Hospital. Kerry and the boys were transported to nearby Summerville Medical Center. Meanwhile Elizabeth was on the phone, enlisting prayer support from our church friends, and she was passing information as she received it. More than anything she wanted to be with our daughter in the emergency room, but MS paralysis prevented it. She's grateful that a friend from our church filled that role for her.

Michael sustained multiple injuries, the worst of which were a crushed ankle and broken knee. His recovery, still ongoing, has included five surgeries with more to come, recurring blood clots, physical therapy, loss of work and pain.

For Kerry, scans of her neck revealed a cracked vertebra, which required six weeks in a hard neck brace to heal. During that time, a friend and her daughter came to their house every afternoon to meet Andrew and Logan at the school bus stop, help them with their homework, and prepare supper for the family. They always made sure Andrew and Logan were off to bed before they left. This was especially helpful to Kerry, who couldn't even look down to see what the boys were doing much less look after her husband and herself.

The boys suffered seat belt burns and some bruises, but were otherwise unhurt. They all relive the memory whenever they face an oncoming car on a curve in the road.

Reason to Rejoice:

Events like this come as perpendicular intrusions. Dropping like bombs, they upend lives, and send schedules and plans careening in all directions. They force-think us beyond day-to-day events to realize we may not be as in control as we once thought. We make plans—as we ought—but our plans carry no guarantee of fulfillment. Therein lies fear of the unexpected, unless, of course, we prepare for it.

Michael was preparing.

Two weeks before the accident, Michael was at the Army Air Assault School at Fort Benning, Georgia, in preparation for a year-long deployment to Afghanistan in February. There, his 40-year-old body competed with 20-somethings and passed the physically rigorous course, an accomplishment he was rightfully proud of.

Prepared for battle, he had no idea the kind of battle he was about to face, but the preparation served him well for his year-long fight to recover.

More than physically, Michael was preparing spiritually with a growing relationship with Jesus Christ. He knew James 1:2-3, *"Consider it all joy, my brethren, when you encounter various trials, knowing that the testing of your faith produces endurance."*

That was one of the Scripture passages Michael used at a talk, "Rejoice in Suffering?" he gave to his unit of the South Carolina National Guard. He told them he certainly had the choice to say, "Why me? Why my family? But the fact is, it is me and it is my family. I have times when I wish it hadn't happened," he said, "but I have to endure the ordeal and know that God will use this to bring us all closer to Him."

Michael IV, for a high school assignment, wrote about the accident and his vivid memory of the violent crash and sound of crushing metal, his uncertainty of his father's condition, and the help he and his family received from his church and friends.

In the essay he wrote: "We were hit by a drunk driver, who already had two DUI convictions, so this was his third. I look back on this event and realize how much this had changed my family's daily life. My dad had planned to be deployed to Afghanistan on February 13, 2011. I realize that if this accident had not occurred, then he would be in Afghanistan for 15 months.

"He continues to have much pain in his ankle still. I did not receive injuries, nor did my brothers. My mom has now fully recovered. I look back and realize this was the hardest year of my life, but my family has survived it. We are stronger and closer than before. Now we can look back and realize this accident turned out to be a blessing."

So, what have we learned? We learned that lessons are best taught when we patiently embrace them. We learned the importance of family who kept us close in their prayers while separated by miles.

And we learned that there's joy in the morning. Morning for the Murphys was a long, slow sunrise, but with the dawn, we see more clearly the hand of God protecting our family in a wreck that could have claimed their lives. That gives us faith to know that his hand is still there, helping us all recover, rebuild, and become what he wants us to be.

Dick Peterson

"Consider it all joy, my brethren, when you encounter various trials, knowing that the testing of your faith produces endurance."

James 1:2-3

CHANGE FROM THE INSIDE OUT

Her afternoons brought fatigue. Elizabeth complained about tingling and a constrictive feeling that made her right leg heavy.

She had falls, one while standing on a chair to hang a poster in her high school classroom. "I should have been more careful," she said. Still, there seemed to be more to it. And there were times when a careless turn caught her off balance and pitched her to the floor where she stayed until I could help lift her. Once, she spent an afternoon on our closet floor waiting until I returned from work.

By this time she had a diagnosis—multiple sclerosis. "It will only get worse. There's no cure," her doctor said bluntly.

This intruder invaded Elizabeth's body, and by extension, mine. Her disease became my disease and made demands on our relationship we were ill-prepared to manage. As she moved from cane to walker to electric scooter and finally to a powered wheelchair, then lost use of her right hand, I had to adjust my life to fit her needs.

Uninvited and unwelcome, this disease now forces us into a kind of sick reality game, leaving no choice but to follow the rules even as they change and become more restrictive.

At night, I help her undress, put on her nightgown, and get her into bed. I bring her hot chocolate, and a handful of pills. In the morning, she depends on me to help her to the bathroom, to bathe, dress for the day, and prepare breakfast with more pills on the side. I shop, cook, wash clothes, set hair, and do many of the things she used to do for herself and me. I'm thankful she's learned to apply mascara, eyeliner, and lipstick with her left hand. And I'm grateful that not one woman in our circle of friends has asked for "hair by Richard," as Elizabeth calls it.

Every family divvies up chores, fairly or not so fairly. The MS dictates ours and it's not at all fair, but we do have the choice to let it tear us apart or use it to strengthen our marriage bond as we face the adversity together. This reaches deeper than deciding who does what. It reaches to feelings, emotions, and attitudes about what we do, what's done to us, and who we are to ourselves and each other.

We both pray for healing. But if we only grieve the loss, we miss the gain—that what this disease does *to* us may also be done *for* us. Even as the MS steals abilities from Elizabeth's life, a healing grows almost undetected inside. When we talk about this, Elizabeth wonders aloud, "Did it really take this to teach me that my soul is more important to God than my body?"

And I ask, "Is this what Jesus meant when he taught his disciples to serve? When he washed their feet, did he look 2,000 years into the future and see me washing my wife's clothes and helping her onto her shower seat to bathe? Did it really take this to teach me compassion?"

Could it be that God in his wisdom and love gives Elizabeth and me this disease to heal us from the inside out in ways he considers far more important than how efficiently nerve signals travel from her brain to her muscles? We pray that Elizabeth will resume her old life; he wants her to assume a new life. We long for change on the outside; he desires change on the inside. We pray for what we want; he answers with what he knows we need.

Is it wrong to want a whole, functioning body? Not at all. But though we focus naturally on the flesh, this disease compels Elizabeth and me to turn our minds to the Spirit. The Apostle Paul said, *"For the mind set on the flesh is death, but the mind set on the Spirit is life and peace"* (Romans 8:6,

88

NASB). Elizabeth and I are still learning the realities of that revelation. She tells me that when she had no choice but to submit to multiple sclerosis, she learned how to submit to her Lord.

And he has made me question whom it is I love.

When I pray for healing, is it for Elizabeth? Or is it because her healing would make life so much easier for me? I challenge, "Aren't you the God who heals? I love her and I want her well." But in the back of my mind I know I also want her healed for me.

In response to my challenge, Jesus asks me as he asked Peter, "Do you love me more than these?" I think, *He wants me to love him more than my wife?* So I reply with Peter's words, "Yes, Lord, You know that I love You."

"Tend My lambs" (John 21:15, NASB), he tells me.

I care for Elizabeth. She's his lamb. Doesn't that show I love him?

But what is he really asking? He's asking if I love him more than these things I say I want, the things I'd have if this disease would just go away. Now my answer's not nearly as glib. Can I actually love God more than my wife, but not more than these things I say I want? They're not bad things: a happy, healthy life together, a stroll on the beach without a wheelchair to become bogged down in the sand, getting to church on time because she can dress herself.

The exposure shames me. Do I love him more than these? This is the love of Matthew 22:37-39 that commands me to love God with all that's within me, with all my heart, soul, and mind, and to love my neighbor— my wife—as I would myself.

Loving what I want for myself isn't even on the list.

It's not in me to love like that, except that God has promised that his love *"has been poured out within our hearts through the Holy Spirit who was given to us"* (Romans 5:5, NASB). God has given me an impossible command, but he has given me the power to obey it.

The intruder still resides in our home, still presents us with new challenges each day, and still teaches us forceful lessons on submission, dependence, service, and a love that endures all things and never fails (1 Corinthians 13:7-8)—even when I fail.

Strange as it may seem, that intruder is beginning to look more and more like a guest.

Dick Peterson

"Love bears all things, believes all things, hopes all things, endures all things. Love never ends. As for prophecies, they will pass away; as for tongues, they will cease; as for knowledge, it will pass away."

I Corinthians 13:7-8

WITH ME THROUGH THE VALLEY

Memory of my childhood dream to one day adopt a child returned when Jim and I saw a 20/20 feature on adopting Romanian orphans. So we discussed it over quite a length of time and we decided that was something we would do together.

After our move to Lynchburg, Virginia, a friend from our former church in Maryland told me a group from that church was going to Romania to adopt, and asked if we would like to join them. So we made the connection and I joined in with that group. There was a group of 19 that went over to Romania in March of 1991. I went and Jim stayed home with our three natural born children who were 2, 6, and 8. I was in Romania for 68 days dealing with the Romanian government and the American government. I saw a lot of miraculous answers to prayer during that time and so did Jim. We each kept a journal. We were cared for by our church community.

On May 26, 1991, I returned with our adopted son, Jimmy. We had Jimmy in our family for five years until May 1, 1996. We put him to bed that night and in the morning of May 2, he was lying on the floor, dead.

We called 911. They came and transported him to the hospital where they told us he had expired. We had a funeral for our son, at which time my husband's sister, who was just 13 and had emotional problems, called the police and told them we abused our children. That spurred a four-year investigation. They were investigating me for first-degree murder. The police went to Jim's work and interviewed him separately, trying to pit him against me. They parked in front of our house and went from door to door asking our neighbors what kind of people we were. It actually drew us together and brought us closer as we prayed together.

At that time we had been living in Florida for 10 months and had become involved in a church there. Our church friends in Maryland and Florida prayed for us and when they knew somebody, they called and asked them to pray for this situation. It turned out that there were people praying for us in almost every state in the US, and missionaries in Brazil, Netherlands, and Austria. We had a worldwide prayer chain praying for us through this four-year period. It was all these prayers that held us up and I can say we really did feel the prayer. My mother had sent me what looked like a whole ream of paper filled with Bible promises to help build my faith.

What they finally decided was that there wasn't enough evidence to prosecute. They never came out and said we know you didn't kill your son.

This gives me comfort: Our Jimmy accepted the Lord Jesus as his Savior during the time that we had him. Also, he was in AWANA. Two days before he died he recited John 14:1-6. The year before, he recited the 23rd Psalm. As he died, he knew who was with him and where he was going.

Rita May Ranck

"Let not your hearts be troubled. Believe in God; believe also in me.
In my Father's house are many rooms... And if I go and prepare a place for you, I will come again and will take you to myself, that where I am you may be also."

John 14:1, 3

FROM ANGER TO UNCONDITIONAL LOVE

I was born in 1939 to a violent world and to a sometimes-violent father. One of my first toys was an airplane that dropped bombs—"Bombs Over Berlin."

I attended church every Sunday. I lived in two worlds: a world of old hatred, anger and violence and a Sermon-On-the-Mount world of turn the other cheek.

I came to Crossroads Community Church in 1999 to take a course in Christian Maturity, taught by Hugh Shelbourne. I actually thought I was quite mature.

Hugh had been to Africa in the aftermath of the Hutu and Tutsi massacre where Christians killed each other, much like our own Civil War. I began to see the hypocrisy of claiming Christ-likeness while clinging to anger, resentment and unforgiveness.

I learned that the unconditional love of Christ does not keep an account of wrongs suffered. I learned to leave my gift at the altar and be reconciled to my brother.

My most recent application of my walk from here to there (from where I am as a Christian to where I am moving closer to the Lord), happened a few weeks ago. I had a political dispute with a patient, which was unprofessional. He became angry and stormed out of my office. I immediately wrote letter of apology and he immediately wrote a letter of apology back.

I am reconciled to my brother, who is still my patient.

Dr. John Sanders

"Love ... does not seek its own,
is not provoked,
does not take into account
a wrong suffered."

I Corinthians 13:4-5

NOWHERE TO TURN WITHOUT GOD

Dec. 2, 2009, was a bad day. I was a prison guard when two death row inmates pulled weapons, stabbed me, and left me for dead in a pool of blood. They saw me get up, and followed me to the door. The Lord led me out.

I laughed about what happened, determined not to let one incident keep me from the job I considered a first step to a career in law enforcement. I thought once the 14 stab wounds healed, I'd be back at Lieber Correctional Institution, a level-three prison in Ridgeville, S.C. But in the weeks and months that followed, emotional wounds erased that plan and alienated me from the two places I considered safe—home and church.

I went to church a few weeks later. In the lobby of Crossroads Community Church, a friend approached me from behind, touched me on the shoulder, and told me he was glad to see me. I was gripped with a sudden terror–cold sweats and nausea. I wanted to sink into the wall. Loud noise, a sudden motion, and nightmares of the attack triggered violent responses. I was diagnosed with post-traumatic stress disorder (PTSD).

After two years and with counseling, I thought I was ready to get back to work. I signed for a diesel mechanics course in Pennsylvania, and instead of praying about it, I went ahead and rented an apartment out of state to take the course.

On my way from the class to the apartment, I got lost. I had a breakdown. Five miles from my destination, I was overcome with anxiety and crying. I called my wife, Kim, and a counselor from church. PTSD left me with nowhere to turn without God's direction.

Kim and I see a slow steady recovery. I take medication for anxiety and have learned to do what God puts in front of me—mostly volunteering at church. I was able to use my experience to help a friend recover from a confrontation with an armed intruder.

When I recount the worst of my wounds, I'm amazed at the near-surgical precision in the random stabs. One to my arm cut a tendon but missed an artery. Another to my chest hit the sternum but missed my heart or a lung. One to my face hit less than an inch from an eye, and one to the neck just missed a major artery.

God was in control then, and He is now. It helps to know God is using the attack to help me help someone else.

Nate Sasser

Blessed be the God and Father of our Lord Jesus Christ, the Father of mercies and God of all comfort, who comforts us in all our affliction, so that we may be able to comfort those who are in any affliction, with the comfort with which we ourselves are comforted by God.

2 Corinthians 1:3-4

A VERY PRESENT HELP IN TROUBLE

On October 22, 2010, my husband was admitted to Roper Hospital for surgery to remove a kidney that had a malignant tumor. It was to be a rather safe operation, in that they knew about his diabetes, his heart congestion, and other issues. He should come home in two weeks, they said.

From the get-go, he had problems after the operation due to his chronic obstructive pulmonary disease (COPD) which he had apparently not taken seriously. They sent him to Health South for rehab at the end of the two weeks with instructions he had to use a CPAP machine.

I almost lost him a couple of times during this two-week period. Although Pastor Peppy did not know me at the time, I contacted him and asked him to come talk to my husband at Health South because I knew he was not saved. Peppy came right away and talked to him, but he was not willing to give his heart to Jesus at that time.

I don't know why.

He was back in ICU within three days—in and out of ICU for the next four weeks. One night, after I had made a trip home to change, on the way out I picked up a devotional to read. While all was quiet and I was reading my devotional, my husband started asking me questions about my faith and the Lord. I turned to a place in my devotional that aided me in leading him to the Lord.

My heart burst with joy.

Although they had been unable to get him up out of the bed, at the end of the six weeks, they said they could do nothing else for him and released him to go. We arrived around 5 p.m. The next morning was quiet but around two o'clock Physical Therapy came in to get him up. He told them he did not feel well at least twice but they told him, they had to get him up into the wheelchair.

Before they could seat him in the chair, he had a pulmonary embolism and died immediately. It was quite a shock to me and hard to believe, but the one thing I know is that he is with the Lord, which is a blessed comfort.

My testimony is this: God has used me to minister to other people, especially those battling cancer and loss of a spouse. He has given me the ability to accomplish what his plan is for me. I pray that he will continually use me as he wants.

"Trust in the Lord with all your heart, and do not lean on your own understanding. In all your ways acknowledge him, and he will make straight your paths" (Proverbs 3:5-6).

Linda Sealy

"God is our refuge and strength, a very present help in trouble. Therefore we will not fear though the earth gives way, though the mountains be moved into the heart of the sea..."

Psalm 46:1-2

GOD AT THE CENTER

Years ago, Vinny, the man who would become my husband, was in a much different place than me. He had been divorced for several years and was very lonely. He asked God either to bring him a soulmate or change his heart so that he wouldn't desire a mate. He asked the men in his accountability group at church to join him in prayer for God's answer.

Unlike Vinny, I had dealt with all the pain I had ever intended to deal with in a marital relationship. After my divorce, I built walls to protect myself. I told myself I was content with my life, and I surrounded myself with some wonderful Christian girlfriends who had a heart for God. Each had her own battles, but the love of Christ was the common thread that ran through the group.

One night, I was at a ladies' Bible study with both of my daughters. Mia, who led the study, was known to pray whatever she felt the Lord was impressing on her. That evening she prayed for me. She asked God to place a godly man of his choice in my life. I was so caught off guard I opened my eyes in shock! The last thing I told God about a man was that I was done. Then it hit me, my girls were there. What were they thinking? This was not my prayer. Why did she pray this? I did not want my girls thinking that I wanted a man. I was content with my life.

When I asked my daughter Megan, she laughed and said Mia prayed whatever God laid on her heart. She seemed okay with the prayer and told me her sister Brooke was praying the exact same prayer for me. Well, that was their prayer, not mine.

About a month later, when my dear friend Tamara, who was just days away from being married, asked me what characteristics I would like to see in a guy I would date. I assured her that I was not interested in dating

103

so it did not apply to me. She insisted that the list was just for fun, so I wrote out a list in my journal and tossed her the list to read. She laughed and said there was not a man alive who could meet those standards and I was just trying to protect myself. I knew there was truth in what she said, but I truly was not interested in dating. I had always told my girls, unless you are looking to get married, there was no reason to date, and I was not ready nor had any intentions of getting ready.

Mutual friends of Vinny and I held their annual all-day, come and go as you like pig pickin'. When Brooke and I left after having lunch there, I grabbed my cooler without knowing there was a two-liter soda inside. Since we would be going close to the pig pickin' on our way to the church that night, I decided to drop the soda off on our way.

When we arrived to return the soda, Vinny was there. Our mutual friend insisted that we needed to meet each other, so we talked. I will never forget the words that our friend used to describe Vinny: "He is a man of modest means, but great integrity." I had never met anyone who was described to me that way. Integrity means the quality of being honest and having strong moral principles. Due to the issues that destroyed my marriage, I wanted to see what this person was all about.

Our first date occurred on Friday, July 15. As I was getting ready that evening and talking with my daughter about my fears, Brooke hugged me and prayed that God would give me a peace and an enjoyable evening.

Over dinner, Vinny shared the list of things he was looking for in someone. That got my attention as I thought of my list, but I did not share mine with him. I was guarded with the things I said that evening and let him do the talking. This gave me an opportunity to sort my thoughts and be aware of the sense of peace I felt. This was exactly what Brooke had prayed.

The next day, Vinny asked me in a text if I had read the devotional for that day. I had not. He said it was about the church being a hospital for hurting divorced people, a place of healing and growing in the Lord. He said that he would get me one the next day, but the scripture reference was Proverbs 18:22. He had only read the devotion, but not the Scripture reference.

I found the reference and Brooke was looking over my shoulder as I read it: *"He who finds a wife finds a good thing and obtains favor from the LORD."* Brooke gasped and said, "Oh, my." I was not sure what to think but since it had been such a lovely evening the night before, I didn't want to jump to conclusions. I'd wait to see what the devotion said. In the meantime, when Vinny looked up the scripture, he thought he had blown it.

To this day, other than God's good sense of humor, we're still not sure what that scripture has to do with that devotion.

This was just the beginning of God's confirmation of his work in our relationship and bringing us together for his glory. We quickly realized that Ephesians 3:20 was at work in our lives: *"Now to him who is able to do far more abundantly than all that we ask or think, according to the power at work within us."* We always think that we need to be content, but in my case, being content was not God's plan for my life. I needed to seek out the best that he had for my life.

When I was not able to pray for a relationship, God had others praying on my behalf for Vinny. There has been healing in both of our lives because, in both cases, there was great pain from a broken covenant. My biggest issue was a lack of trust. Vinny's biggest issue was a sense of worthlessness. Having open and honest communication allowed us to know where we were wounded and how to cover those areas in prayer.

Vinny received great counsel from his pastor. He cautioned Vinny to set boundaries in "touch." Certain forms of touch are not appropriate, but where do you draw the line when touch is your love language? Vinny wanted to be careful to know for certain what God's will was for our relationship. Because of that, he explained to me how he felt about where we were in our relationship, but that he needed to be careful even about holding hands. Our mutual friend kept asking if he had held my hand yet. She just could not understand why that mattered, but God knew, because it was my love language too.

As Vinny allowed God to direct him, Vinny also protected me. Vinny was being a godly leader, respecting me, and it was drawing me closer. This caused me to think back about my list and I realized that Vinny was everything I listed.

God was the center of our relationship. Ecclesiastes 4:12b says *"a threefold cord is not quickly broken"* and I felt that was God's foundation for us for doing things His way.

As we went through premarital counseling, we found we were more connected than we knew. Because we chose to do things God's way and not our own way, our spiritual and physical draw to each other was confirmed over and over. As in any relationship, it takes work and a determination to do things God's way. Our focus is to not just remain married but to allow God to grow us and use us.

When God brought us together, he restored two broken people. When God restored the fortunes of Job, he gave him twice as much. When God healed us, he gave us in our marriage immeasurably more than we could have imagined. He has allowed us to use the areas where we experienced our greatest hurt to minister to other hurting couples. What the enemy means for evil, God uses for good.

Vinny and Chrissy Silva

106

"Now to him who is able to do far more abundantly than all that we ask or think, according to the power at work within us."

Ephesians 3:20

FROM PRIDE TO REPENTANCE

On the day we learned of the earthquake at Port-au-Prince, I told my wife that I would likely go with a disaster relief team to Haiti. News reports over the next days were increasingly alarming. Tens of thousands of people had died and hundreds of thousands were stranded with nothing, including medical care. Many well-intentioned medical professionals had immediately flown into the capital city with their equipment and medicines. But after a few days, their food and medicines gone, they had retreated to the airport and become refugees themselves, marooned on the tarmac; their very presence had tragically compromised incoming support.

When my team was called, there were no direct flights to Port-au-Prince. We spent a day on a dusty bus, bouncing along from Santo Domingo to the earthquake zone. I was already winded when we arrived at the Florida Baptist missionary station that evening. The walled compound was in a residential area. It sheltered the only building still standing in a crowded neighborhood of pancaked, cinderblock houses, crushed cars, downed utility lines and collapsed stone walls. Everything was cement gray and the people were living outside on rocks. I had been a doctor in Haiti before – it was badly broken then and the earthquake had not improved the place.

The front porch of our barracks was unstable; the interior was crowded with volunteers like me – engineers, well-drillers, electricians and medical people from all across the U.S. Many were retired white-hairs who had been inspired by the 9-11 events to meet FEMA qualifications and be ready for the next time. We were cramped in small rooms with too many double bunks and served Creole meals by native staff hired by our hosts, a disaster response coordination team. The daily medical work was difficult and I was glad to loosen my boots each evening.

I quickly fell into a routine in the crowded society of strangers. I kept my gear orderly and under the bunk, ate trail mix instead of the thick, spicy food and bathed during the evening meal. I shaved in the early morning, before the others stirred.

In the dark of one morning, I found the little bathroom empty and slipped inside. I noticed the odor, then realized that the floor, the tub and the toilet were generously speckled with the contents of some volunteer's stomach. Too much *manje Ayisien* for supper, I supposed.

I am experienced in third world medicine and have found that I risk my equanimity if I ignore a minimal standard of sanitation and hygiene. A personal failure could then neutralize me and I would become a burden—another victim in an endless wash of victims. Dealing with a medical mess was part of the work and necessary to keep the standard, so I walked over to our hosts who were intently working on their computers near a window. The glow from the screens was the only light.

"The bathroom's a mess – someone threw up in there last night."

"We know. The girl will take care of it."

That was it. That was it? I felt anger rise as I turned and began a search for the materials I would need for the project. The Haitians were suffering enough without having to clean up some American's mess.

I found a closet with the stuff, returned to the bathroom, cleaned up the partially digested remnants of stewed tomato, onion, peppers, garlic and pinto beans and sprinkled a little extra Clorox around. I left the bathroom in order for the next person and began to think through my anger. I was mad at the guy who didn't clean up his own mess. I was mad at the leaders who knew about it and delegated to the Haitian attendant. Mostly, I was mad at American arrogance overseas.

With daylight, we were delayed in leaving for our makeshift clinic (a roofless church near a large refugee camp). I was packing medicines when an elderly Alabama volunteer approached and asked if I might be a doctor. Her husband was upstairs sick and she asked if I might help.

My patient was in his late seventies. He tried to be welcoming as he told me he became sick last night and was too weak to get out of his bunk. Cramps and vomiting, he said. Really bad last night. Could barely crawl back to his bunk from the bathroom. Hated to bother me.

I listened, asked some questions…examined him. "You are dehydrated" I said to him. "But I think the worst has passed. If you can sip fluids and hold them down during the day, I think you'll be okay." He thanked me and asked if he could say a brief prayer for me, before I left for the day. On my way out, I found some oral rehydration fluids, spoke with his wife and joined my team in the truck.

As we bounced across the ruins of Port-au-Prince, I felt the warmth of shame creeping across the back of my neck; then I wiped away a tear. I was wrong to blame him; I was wrong to blame them. It was my pride that troubled me – not theirs. In silence, I confessed *"If I deliver my body to be burned, but do not have love, it profits me nothing"* (1 Corinthians 13:3).

Ed West

"If I deliver my body to be burned,

but do not have love,

it profits me nothing"

1 Corinthians 13:3

PRAISING HIM IN THE STORM

In mid-September Mary took me to the emergency room because I had shortness of breath and I just wasn't feeling well. They put me at the head of the line and gave me oxygen.

I remember they took all my clothes and gave me one of those wonderful hospital gowns that kind of tie in the back, but not always. You know you have to have somebody re-tie it once in awhile and keep it on you, or it exposes you to the outside world.

During the next four weeks, I underwent surgery to replace four coronary arteries. While I was there, I would come in and out of consciousness. There was nothing I could do, and I really didn't know what was going on, so I prayed for guidance and wisdom for the doctors, nurses and staff to do the right thing to help me get better. That was one of my prayers.

My second prayer was for my family; they underwent the stress. I was kept sedated most of the time and I can tell you I didn't suffer one bit with the exception of knowing my family was under a lot of stress. I would wake up at times to hear their voices and it was a good feeling. I had a lot of people — not just from our church, but friends and people all around — who would come to the waiting room and pray. I was told that by my family, and it was wonderful to hear.

My third prayer was for a brand-new John Deere tractor. My son and I have been using this 1956 Ford tractor. We've been thinking of upgrading on that tractor.

It's great that the prayers were answered with the doctors and staff. Wisdom from God took over, and guided them to what they needed to do. Without God, I wouldn't be here talking about it today.

The second answer to prayer was that peace I got when I knew my family was being taken care of. We had a lot of family come in from out of town. That relieved Mary from having to be here at the house and let her spend more time with me. It brought me peace to become conscious of Mary holding my hand and then listen to her pray.

The Scripture I thought about in the hospital was James 1:2— *"Count it all joy, my brothers, when you meet trials of various kinds, for you know that the testing of your faith produces steadfastness."* It kept coming back into my mind. I just turned that all over to him and I could feel that peace. As I drifted in and out of consciousness, I knew it was okay.

I know that when I accepted Jesus as my Lord and Savior and considered what he did at the cross for me, I got a different gown, and the tie in the back is Jesus. We all as Christians receive that gown when we accept him and Jesus is the one thing we all have in common. All the people praying for me around the country, in the church, in the waiting room—people I didn't even know and churches I'd never been in—they are the tie that binds all of us together. We're very blessed to have such a great Christian family all over the country and at Crossroads.

The other Scripture I had was Phil. 4:6-7. *"Do not be anxious about anything, but in everything by prayer and supplication with thanksgiving let your requests be made known to God. And the peace of God, which surpasses all understanding, will guard your hearts and your minds in Christ Jesus."* And that was the peace I received and we received as a family. It's just a wonderful feeling when you turn it all over to him.

And about that John Deere, we're still driving the 1956 Ford tractor. But that's just stuff in our lives and it doesn't count for anything.

I had it easy. When I came to and they told me I had four coronary bypasses, I was ready to bet my house I didn't. All I feel are the stitches in my chest. I've had no pain whatsoever. According to Mary they nearly lost me twice. All the credit goes to God.

Jay Williams

I want to add a little "wife perspective" of what was going on in the waiting rooms and critical care unit (CCU) for almost four weeks.

On September 17 Jay went to the hunting property with a couple of hunters and spent the whole morning and afternoon working on food plots with them. We were dealing with doctors for over a month and each one had said that their specialty was not the one that was causing his shortness of breath and fatigue. We were advised to go to primary care physician since it was not endocrine, nephrology, or blood.

The appointment that would have discovered the heart blockages was five days away when he left the house that morning feeling pretty good. He remembers having a great time driving his '56 Ford tractor and riding on a four-wheeler with some youngsters before he started feeling poorly. By 7 o'clock he and I were at Summerville Medical Center waiting for an ambulance to take us to Trident Heart. I was stunned. I never suspected heart.

Both of our children and their families were together at Clemson that weekend for a nursing event for our granddaughter Summer, and for a football game. When I called them at 9 o'clock, they were all together in a lake house and they immediately made plans to return to Summerville at dawn and began praying together.

Our daughter who lives in Atlanta traveled back with her husband to their home and picked up her car and headed to us. Bryan was at Trident by noon, Wendy at 3:30. They never left me or Jay again, and we stayed in his room in the CCU during every allowed hour and minute.

The three of us watched them intubate Jay and put him to sleep as his poor heart and lungs were so congested that he was not going to survive unless they did the work for him. We had five days of their struggling to get the lungs clear enough for a heart catheter and at the same time running a form of dialysis which removes fluid from the body and replaces it with less fluid: Continuous Renal Replacement Therapy (CRRT).

Our grandson Garrett, sang "Just a Closer Walk With Thee," and sent it by phone so that each night we would play it in Jay's ear before we left him. He doesn't remember much of what went on in CCU, but Bryan, Wendy, and I will never forget those days when we prayed courage into each other.

Ed West (Doc) appeared and disappeared so many times through those days. Peppy too. Each time they started a new procedure or added a tube or line, Doc would explain the significance of it, in detail, and then spend time in prayer with us and over Jay. What peace that gave us!

I do remember one time sitting in the waiting room—it might have been the day of the heart catheter. I talked to Pep and Doc about my fears that I was not abiding by Jay's wishes in his living will, because of all the tubes and the machinery that was keeping him alive. I remember saying that I don't want to see him survive all this and be mad at me because we allowed him to live only to need oxygen, dialysis, and a wheelchair. I

115

don't remember how they reassured me, but I do know that I decided to trust God to take Jay to be with him, if that was what He wanted to do. That would be fine, because Jay had already lived out his testimony, and I knew God would take care of us who would survive.

We had so many people appear and disappear, bringing snacks, notes, and always the prayers. We found amazing nurses and doctors who allowed us to pray for them and prayed with us.

At home, Wendy, our daughter-in-law Peggy, and the granddaughters cared for the two mothers, mine and Jay's, both 96 years old. Our Sunday school class brought them meals every day. Each night Wendy and I would journey back to Trident for the 8:30-to-10 visiting hours in CCU and there we would have an opportunity to comfort each other. We would search the Word for what we were praying for that day, for lungs to clear, kidneys to function better, the heart catheter procedure that had to be done, for Jay to be strong enough for surgery (that happened 13 days after we went to Trident). Those specific prayers were answered, one by one.

Jay was out of surgery and still waiting for kidneys to decide to function or not when Hurricane Matthew came through. By then we were out of CCU and on the 3rd floor of Trident, so I was allowed to stay with him in his room 24 hours. We rode out the storm together. I posted to friends that we would be "Praising Him in the Storm." And we did!

Mary Williams

116

"Count it all joy, my brothers, when you meet trials of various kinds, for you know that the testing of your faith produces steadfastness."

James 1:2

LEANING ON JESUS

"Keep your head in the air, your feet on the ground, and you can't put your foot in your mouth!" That was how I used to sign off my radio show in the 1970s.

Broadcasting at a Christian radio station while in high school was my part time job and that opened the door for overseeing the Fourth Marine Air Wing sound studio during my military service. My duty included recording programs that were used across the U.S. to promote the Marine Corps. For about 25 years I worked as a DJ, program director, sales manager and eventually station manager at both secular and Christian radio stations in several states. I loved broadcasting and in particular Christian radio and the opportunity it gave me to encourage fellow believers and to share the good news of Jesus with the community.

In 1991, I became station manager of a Christian radio station in Augusta, Georgia. It was exciting living in Augusta during The Master's each year. Being a member of the press afforded me the opportunity to spend The Masters at the course giving live reports to our audience. It also made it possible for me to play the course several times. In fact, the last time I played golf was at the Augusta National Golf course.

All of that came to a screeching halt in 1994 when I was diagnosed with multiple sclerosis. I'm sure I had multiple sclerosis for years but two things made me go to the doctor. I was having trouble with my balance and my lip was drawing up making me feel like I was sneering. I thought my balance was being affected by an inner ear infection, but I did not understand the "sneering." My doctor recommended that I go to a neurologist. The diagnosis was fairly quick—multiple sclerosis. For a few years managing the symptoms was doable while still working.

When my diagnosis became public many folks reached out to me wanting to help. The Christian radio station audience sent me hankies they had prayed over, and invited me to come to their church to be healed. They meant well, but ultimately they decided my faith was weak because I was not healed. I believe God has the power to heal, but in my case God has decided not to heal the disease. I also believe he never leaves us or forsakes us, and he gives me the strength to live with my disease.

There was an arrangement with the owner of the radio station to allow me to purchase the station, but a year or so after my diagnosis he decided to sell the radio station to someone else. On December 31, 1995, I went into work and found the station had been sold. A new owner was to take over at midnight and I was told my services would no longer be needed. I was devastated. Broadcasting had been all I'd known for years.

At my next doctor's appointment, I shared about my job situation and the doctor encouraged me to file for Social Security disability due to my declining health. I'd heard the war stories about filing for disability and the length of time it took to get approved. I was struggling with some issues that made it difficult to work. I couldn't lift and carry weight which most of the jobs listed in the paper required.

What was I going to do to supply for the needs of my wife and family? I knew that unemployment would last only a few months. Looking back, I can see God's hand at work through these events in providing for my family. My unemployment ran out in June of that year and disability kicked in July 1. I realized more than ever before that my heavenly Father was truly in charge of everything going on in and around me, and I could trust him.

As I began reading about MS, I learned there were several types including relapse-remitting and primary progressive, which I have. Relapse-remitting is when you receive an MS attack, which may keep you out of work, but eventually you feel better and go back to work. The only problem is after the attack you may not go back to where you were. With each attack your health is declining. With primary progressive MS, there is a steady gradual decline in your abilities and in your health.

Multiple sclerosis is a cruel disease and affects different people different ways. Many folks suffer a burning, tingling, or a numbness in their arms or legs like I did in my left side. Balance for me always seemed to be affected. When you first start living with MS it's easy for people to think you have been drinking because of your unsteady gait.

At first, living with MS seemed pretty easy. I used to tell friends that if you had to have a disease, MS was a good one to have. The longer I live with it, and my physical body declines, the harder everything becomes. I remember back in the beginning trying to figure out what was in a cardboard box. I reached in and tried to pull out whatever was in it only to discover it was broken glass. I didn't know it, but I had been cutting my hand on the broken glass. Because of the MS I didn't feel the pain. MS also affects your body when it comes to temperatures, and the heat of summer often makes symptoms worse.

History had intrigued me for years but I had not had time to pursue this interest. Once I became disabled I had lots of time to read and explore the rich history of our area. I found myself spending hours studying history, talking with historians and learning about Augusta's past. This led me to opportunities to become a docent at the Woodrow Wilson boyhood home in Augusta, the Ezekiel Harris House, the Augusta Museum, and to give tours for the Augusta Visitor's Bureau. It was like a dream come true.

In 2006 we sold our home in Augusta and moved to Summerville, South Carolina. I was walking with the aid of a cane. I had a couple of falls so I started using a walker. The Ralph H. Johnson VA Medical Center downtown Charleston became my home away from home as my MS symptoms increased. In 2008 the VA provided me a power chair and built a ramp for our home. I am extremely grateful for the good care I have received from the VA. We were able to buy a used 2002 Dodge Ram van with a power lift.

Summerville provided a whole new area to explore. The first several years I spent my days learning all I could about the history of our new home. I started Summerville Tours and provided guided tours for folks interested in the history of our area. The tours ended when my mobility became more challenging. All the notes and information gleaned from years of research in Augusta and Summerville provided the material needed to write three books about these areas and have given me hours of enjoyment.

Living with MS confined to a power chair has its negatives and positives. First, the negatives. When family or friends want to give you a hug, it's hard when you're sitting in the chair. When you want to reach dishes in the cabinet, it's hard. If you want to reach food in the microwave or the refrigerator, it's hard. It's hard when you discover that everyday living is hard. But with the negatives come the positives. I don't know how many times I've seen children watching me as I'm lowered in my chair out of the van. It looks like great fun. My grandchildren love to stand on the lift and ride up and down.

As a young boy I took Proverbs 3:5-6 as my life verses: *"Trust in the Lord with all your heart and lean not on your own understanding. In all your ways acknowledge Him and He shall direct your path."* Living with MS has taught me to lean heavily on my Father. My understanding of why I have this disease is far from clear, but I do acknowledge that if I keep my eyes focused on him, he will continue to direct my path.

Mark Woodard

121

"Trust in the Lord with all your heart and lean not on your own understanding. In all your ways acknowledge Him and He shall direct your path."

Proverbs 3:5 & 6

REMINDERS OF GOD'S PROVISION

In 1993 our family was preparing for another transition. That's pretty much what life is made up of – one transition after another. To me it seems you get life under control and a new transition shakes the norm.

At the age of 40, I'd spent 19 of those years raising children. The oldest was in college and contemplating marriage and the other 3 were in high school. To say it was a busy household is an understatement. The kids were all involved in athletics, had jobs, and worked in our church, besides the normal school obligations. I was handling the business side of the radio station my husband managed. For much of our married life I helped him with various businesses he owned.

In the fall of 1993, I noticed my husband's watch was often on the column shifter in his car instead of on his wrist. When I asked him about it he shrugged it off saying that he just felt funny sometimes wearing it. Around that same time we were shopping and I noticed he kept stumbling and eventually grabbed my shoulder to steady himself as he walked. He shrugged this off too as an inner ear issue. After some wifely nagging, he agreed to see a doctor. Within a couple of months he was diagnosed with multiple sclerosis.

Over the course of the next year I felt an urging of the Lord to pursue a job away from the radio station. At first Mark was totally opposed to the idea but eventually gave in. When a position opened in our church office, I jumped at it. The position provided medical insurance for our family and an extra income. Within a year of starting the job, Mark's position at the radio station ended and he was forced to go on disability.

I was raised in a Christian home, the oldest child of missionaries to Liberia, West Africa, where I spent 10 years of my early life. At the age of 5, I accepted Jesus as my personal savior. Time and time again he had proven faithful to me but I often struggled with fear. 2 Timothy 1:7: *"God has not given us a spirit of fear, but a spirit of power and love and a sound mind"* became my mantra as I faced unfamiliar places, people and things throughout my adolescence and teen years. Even as an adult I was not one to venture out, take risks or feel comfortable on my own.

With Mark's disability, my role dramatically changed as I became the breadwinner and caregiver. I had to step out of my comfort zone. Fear gripped me often in the early years of his diagnosis when we struggled financially with three in college and medical bills that were escalating. In 2006 I was offered a job at a Christian school in North Charleston, S.C. It would mean a major move for Mark and me, but as we prayed about it, we truly felt that it was a door God was opening for us. By then our children had all graduated from college and started families of their own.

As I began my new job, Mark began digging into the rich history of our new surroundings and loved exploring during the day while I was working, and on the weekends. We enjoyed going to the beach in the late afternoon and walking and listening to sounds of the waves. Mark also got connected with the Veterans Administration Hospital and clinics in Charleston. For the first time since his diagnosis, we were able to get the medical bills under control.

One day when I came home from work, I found Mark had fallen. Thankfully he was not seriously hurt but the fall began a downward spiral. Up to that point he had been mobile with a cane. For the next three months, his falls became more frequent and it wasn't unusual to find him on the ground unable to get up when I got home. He ended up in the hospital and was treated with steroids, but when he came home, it was in a wheel chair.

God's faithfulness to us was real and tangible. One day I was sharing with a coach at our school, who also was a car salesman, the fact that we would be looking for a handicap accessible vehicle shortly because of Mark's condition. Not long after Mark came home in the wheelchair, I received an email with a picture of a handicap accessible van that was for sale with very low mileage. I was so thankful to not have to load and unload a manual chair into the trunk of our car anymore. This provision was a tangible reminder to both of us of God's faithfulness and care about the details of our life.

Today life is very different. Walking on the beach is no longer doable, but we have a pond in our back yard with lots of wild life and a small deck which brings Mark pleasure. Even though Mark is no longer able to drive, he has taken the information he learned from exploring, when we first moved to the area, to write a book. We enjoy traveling to visit our children and their families when possible. Transitions constantly keep us on our toes. We are learning to adapt to meet new challenges in Mark's health. But the one thing we both know is that God will be there in the new challenge just like he has been in the past.

Cindy Woodard

"The Lord himself goes before you and will be with you; he will never leave you nor forsake you. Do not be afraid; do not be discouraged"

Deuteronomy 31:8

41575743R00073

Made in the USA
Middletown, DE
18 March 2017